THE
BRITISH
MUSEUM

SOUVENIR

GUIDE

First published in 2003 by The British Museum Press
A division of The British Museum Company Ltd
46 Bloomsbury Street, London WC1B 3QQ

Some of the material in this book was previously published
in *The British Museum*, 1997 and 2000.

ISBN 0-7141-2782-5

Designed by LewisHallam

Printed in Belgium
by Proost NV

COVER ILLUSTRATIONS
Main illustration: Sarcophagus of Sasobek, vizier (prime minister) of the northern
part of Egypt during the reign of Psammetichus I, 26th Dynasty. Siltstone, c. 630 BC.
Details (left to right): Athenian black-figure amphora (p. 70); Assyrian relief (p. 16);
the Battersea Shield (p. 67); the Portland Vase (p. 76); Aztec/Mixtec mosaic serpent (p. 57).

Title page: Wall painting from the tomb of Nebamun, Thebes (p. 33).
Above: The Royal Gold Cup (p. 83)
Opposite: The goddess Tara (p. 44)

THE BRITISH MUSEUM

SOUVENIR GUIDE

Contents

Introduction

The British Museum celebrates the 250th anniversary of its foundation in 2003. Its principal aims today are to be at the centre of international scholarship and to disseminate knowledge for the education, in the widest sense of the word, of all. This is achieved through display at the Museum, and elsewhere by loans, a vigorous programme of lectures and seminars, and publication in large numbers of articles and books. From its earliest days in the eighteenth century, the Museum collected, displayed, stored and preserved the works of humankind (and, at that time, the works of nature too) with great earnestness. This was the Age of Enlightenment and, as the author of the first Museum guide wrote in 1761, 'Curiosity almost universally prevails . . . Nothing can conduce more to preserve the Learning which this latter Age abounds with, than having Repositories in every Nation to contain its Antiquities, such as is the Museum of Britain.'

The British Museum has never simply been a museum of antiquities of Britain. In fact, for its first century of existence, rather little of British origin was collected. From the very beginning, interests were universal, and though fashions in collecting can be detected over the years, the

collection as it exists today must be the most balanced, in terms of world cultures and chronology, that exists anywhere. The collections are vast. For many of its temporary exhibitions, the Museum does not need to borrow; it can simply dip into its remarkable reserves to treat subjects as diverse as gold from South America, the culture of the Maldives, Rembrandt drawings and Hindu religion.

The founding collection was formed by Sir Hans Sloane, a physician by profession and an antiquarian by inclination. Born in 1660, Sloane was, from the first, devoted to scientific enquiry. After a spell in the West Indies, he wrote a book on the natural history of Jamaica. On his return to London, he became a fashionable doctor, which helped to finance his collecting activities.

On Sloane's death in 1753, his collection was counted as containing 79,575 objects, and this did not include the plant specimens in his herbarium and his library of books and manuscripts. He had wanted his collection to be given to King George II for the nation. It was eventually transferred to Parliament after a public lottery raised money for the establishment of the Museum. A late seventeenth-century mansion on the edge of London, Montagu

1

House, was purchased for the purpose by the Board of Trustees, the chairman of which was, by virtue of his office, the Archbishop of Canterbury. The British Museum first opened its doors to the public on 15 January 1759, for 'studious and curious Persons' as they were described. There was no admission fee, but a ticket had to be obtained by somewhat tortuous means, and, once inside, it was necessary to join a guided tour.

The new Museum started to collect enthusiastically, a large proportion of the

2

3

acquisitions being donated. There was a bias towards natural-history specimens in the earliest days, including material collected by Captain James Cook on his circumnavigations of the globe. Ethnographic objects also came from this source. Great Britain was active in voyages of discovery at this time, but Britons were also discovering the classical world on the Grand Tour. Sir William Hamilton, British Envoy in Naples, collected Greek pottery and sent two boatloads to England (though only one of them arrived). It was through Hamilton that the Portland Vase eventually reached the Museum. Charles Townley's celebrated collection of sculpture, amassed in Rome, was sold to the Museum. The defeat of Napoleon's army in Egypt led to the acquisition of the Rosetta Stone and other Egyptian antiquities. In 1816 came perhaps the greatest of all groups of sculptures that would be added to the collections: the fine marbles from the Parthenon in Athens. Lord Elgin had been appointed Ambassador at Constantinople in 1799. Concerned about the destruction of classical remains in Greece, he assembled a team of artists and architects to record what survived and later obtained permission from the authorities to remove carved stone. The sculptures arrived in London in 1802, and Elgin displayed them to the public. In financial difficulty, he sold them to the government fourteen years later, and, when established in the Museum, they immediately created great interest.

British envoys and ambassadors played a significant part in adding to the archaeological collections. In Egypt, the Consul General Henry Salt, with the help of an agent, Giovanni Belzoni, formed a large collection that included much colossal

4

sculpture such as the head of Pharaoh Amenhotep III, purchased by the Museum Trustees in 1823. In 1818, Salt also donated the famous head of Ramesses II. Fascination with the archaeology of the biblical lands spread collecting activities further to the Middle East. Claudius Rich, resident in Baghdad from 1811 to 1820, formed a small collection of inscribed bricks, cylinder seals and engraved tablets from the plains of the Tigris and Euphrates rivers, and in so doing laid the foundation for the Museum's collection of Babylonian and Assyrian antiquities.

By early in the nineteenth century, it was becoming clear that Montagu House was too small for its task. Not only were

the antiquities collections growing rapidly, but the natural history specimens and library were adding to the problem. Additionally, there were pressures from the public, who were coming in increasing numbers; in 1814, the Trustees pointed out that between 28,000 and 30,000 persons had visited the collections in the previous year. The problem came to a head in 1823, when King George IV offered his father's library of nearly 85,000 items to the Museum. A year later, it was decided to erect a new building somewhat to the north of Montagu House, and Sir Robert Smirke was chosen to design it. The form of the new Museum was to consist of side- and top-lit galleries around a large

5

6

courtyard. This was achieved by the early 1840s; the last main part of the building to be constructed was the great portico with its fluted columns and Ionic capitals. As the entrance front grew, so Montagu House was demolished. By 1850, the Museum looked substantially as it does today.

The problems of space were not over, however. The famous Round Reading Room was built in the courtyard garden very shortly afterwards and was open for readers by 1857. The natural history collections were also posing problems, and ultimately it was decided that they should be separated from the artefacts; they moved to South Kensington, in west London, in 1880. Although Smirke's new Museum was still not big enough, a parliamentary commission of 1850 pointed out that some aspects of collecting were being insufficiently attended to. This led to the appointment of Augustus Wollaston Franks, a curator with a considerable breadth of interest and knowledge, who over nearly 50 years built up the collections of post-classical European antiquities, ethnography and Oriental art. By the turn of the twentieth century, the Museum had established the coverage of its collections just as its founders had

hoped it would, though in 1973 the decision was taken to divide the collections again, taking the books and manuscripts to form the new British Library.

What characterises the British Museum today? Most significant is the greater emphasis than hitherto on interpretation. Scholarship in historical and archaeological research, as well as scientific investigation, enable the Museum to adopt a multi-disciplinary approach well suited to its wide-ranging collections.

Perhaps of even greater significance is the importance given by the Museum to the dissemination of that scholarship at many levels and to the widest possible audience, not only within the galleries of the Museum, but far beyond them.

All this is not to say that collecting has been ignored. The late twentieth century was a very active period, in particular with the acquisition of material culture by the Ethnography Department. The Museum has always relied heavily

Learning and Teaching

Relatively few objects enter the collections of the British Museum with their identity certain and their history completely known. It is the task of the Museum to learn as much as possible about each object and its context. Research is mostly undertaken by curators, but vital research work is also carried out by scientists and conservators. In addition, the Museum has an important role as a centre of scholarship for scholars the world over, who come to consult the collections and to exchange information. The Museum is a place of learning in the broadest sense, and all staff have a responsibility to share and disseminate their knowledge to any interested person. The general public and teaching professionals have access to subject experts through correspondence and departmental Student Rooms, and to up-to-date information through lectures, seminars, special exhibitions and extensive publication and education programmes.

7

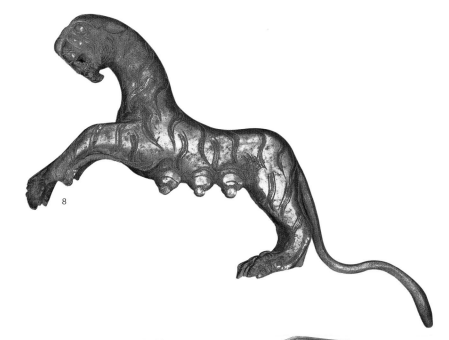

8

9

on private donations and bequests for acquisitions, and now has the additional support of bodies such as the Heritage Lottery Fund, the National Heritage Memorial Fund, the National Art Collections Fund and the British Museum Friends (formerly the British Museum Society).

Fieldwork and excavation are now being pursued more actively than at any other time in the past. The aim of field-work is to conduct research and add material to the collections that is representative of contemporary cultural practices, allowing the Museum to retain its claim to be a museum of world cultures past and present. This aim is largely, but not exclusively, pursued by the Ethno-graphy Department, which has been active in parts of the world as diverse as Romania and New Guinea. Excavations are carried out by the Museum to increase

knowledge and provide an invaluable method of adding new material to the collections, although not all finds come to the Museum. Traditionally, excavations have been carried out by the Museum in the Nile Valley (Egypt and the Sudan) and the Near East, and this important work continues, often in collaboration with other bodies, but the Museum also excavates sites in Britain, as well as in other parts of the world. Evaluation of the discoveries made forms an important part of the work at the Museum; the size and significance of a site can mean that it will take many years to excavate and analyse fully.

The collections are now divided between ten curatorial departments – Ancient Egypt and Sudan, Ancient Near East, Coins and Medals, Ethnography, Greek and Roman Antiquities, Japanese

Antiquities, Medieval and Modern Europe, Oriental Antiquities, Prehistory and Early Europe, and Prints and Drawings – each headed by a Keeper who has overall responsibility for the care, presentation and documentation of the objects. Taken together, the collections of the British Museum make it perhaps the best single introduction to world cultures and civilisations that exists today.

---

5   The head of the chariot horse of Selene (the moon goddess) from the east pediment of the Parthenon in Athens.

6   The Rosetta Stone, one of the Museum's greatest treasures. Egyptian, 196 BC. It provided the key to the decipherment of ancient Egyptian hieroglyphics.

7   Moving the colossal head of Ramesses II to the new Egyptian Sculpture Gallery in 1834.

8   The silver tigress from the Hoxne Treasure. Roman, fourth century AD.

An impressive Roman treasure hoard was found at Hoxne, Suffolk, in 1992. It was acquired by the Museum with help from the National Heritage Memorial Fund, the National Art Collections Fund and the British Museum Society.

9   The 'Franks Casket'. Anglo-Saxon, from Northumbria, England. Whalebone, c. AD 700.

The casket was bought by Augustus Wollaston Franks and presented to the Museum in 1867.

The Great Court

The remarkable new heart of the British Museum, known as the Queen Elizabeth II Great Court, was opened in December 2000. It came about in response to changing needs and demands, and to new opportunities that had arisen. The major part of the Museum had been designed by Smirke in 1823, a time when the maximum annual attendance was around 100,000. By the 1990s the number of visitors in some years exceeded 6 million. The Museum had become uncomfortably overcrowded, and facilities such as teaching rooms, temporary exhibition galleries, shops and restaurants, which were not included in Smirke's brief, were inadequate.

In 1973 the Museum's library departments were separated from the curatorial departments to form the British Library, and in 1998 the Library moved to a new building alongside St Pancras Station, releasing some 40 per cent of the Museum's floor space. The Museum drew up plans to produce a more rational building, allowing for greater ease of circulation and the much-needed new

visitor facilities. Most importantly, the Ethnographic collections could be brought back to Bloomsbury from the Museum of Mankind, the Piccadilly home to which they had been exiled in 1970.

The key to all this was Smirke's courtyard, originally a large garden at the centre of the exhibition galleries. This space had been encroached upon in 1854 with the construction of the British Museum Reading Room, an impressive and inspiring circular room capped by a huge dome, completed in 1857. The Reading Room was built at the centre of the courtyard but all remaining space at the corners had been filled with subsidiary buildings. In drawing up the brief for the architectural competition, launched in 1993, the Trustees stipulated that these other buildings should be cleared away.

The architectural firm chosen to work with the Museum was Foster and Partners. Sir Norman (now Lord) Foster's scheme is an admirably simple concept. A new public space has been created by building a floor around the Reading Room across the courtyard at ground level to connect

1

with the Smirke galleries on all sides. This solves problems of access, circulation and congestion in a straightforward manner. Below ground level are an Education Centre and Ethnographic galleries. Stairways wind round the Reading Room to a new three-storey building attached to its north side, containing shops, an exhibition gallery and, at the uppermost level, a restaurant.

COMPASS: exploring the collections online (www.thebritishmuseum.ac.uk/compass)

COMPASS provides an online guide to the Museum on computer terminals in the Walter and Leonore Annenberg Information Centre in the Reading Room and on the Museum's website.

Around 5,000 objects have been chosen as an introduction to the huge range of the Museum's collections, from gold torcs to contemporary art. Each has a short article illustrated with high-quality images that you can enlarge and study in detail. The system features a wealth of links, background information and maps to help plan your visit. There are online tours on a variety of subjects, including introductions to the current exhibitions, and exciting explanatory animations. You can order high-quality photographic prints of objects as a gift or souvenir.

Also on the website is children's COMPASS (thebritishmuseum.ac.uk/childrenscompass) where

Alfred the British Museum lion welcomes you to a range of information, activities, noticeboards for children's work, competitions and an 'Ask the Expert' feature. For teachers there are high-quality resources linked to the UK National Curriculum.

Text-only versions of both sites provide access for the visually impaired.

From here, a bridge leads to the galleries on the upper floors. An addition to the scheme has been the development of the old North Library, forming the heart of the Ethnography galleries and creating a north–south route through the Museum for the first time. Capping the Great Court is a magnificent, delicate, web-like roof of steel and glass. With its airy heights and vast spaces, the Great Court has become an urban covered square, the first in London, and some striking sculptures from the Museum's collections have been set within it.

The Great Court scheme was financed with grants from the Millennium Commission and the Heritage Lottery Fund. The remaining very considerable sums required were raised by generous donations from corporate, private and anonymous sponsors. Among the new facilities are the Clore Education Centre and its associated Ford Centre for Young Visitors: these welcome thousands of schoolchildren and adults every week and educational programmes have been developed to attract new audiences. The refurbished Reading Room houses the Hamlyn Library and the multi-media programme COMPASS, which enable visitors to make their own discoveries. New galleries include the Joseph Hotung Great Court Gallery (for temporary exhibitions) and the Sainsbury African Galleries.

For the 250th anniversary of the Museum in 2003 its greatest room, the King's Library, is being restored. It was opened in 1827 to house the collection of books created by George III (now in the British Library). A permanent exhibition entitled 'Discovery and Learning in the Age of King George III' will show how studies of nature and of man-made artefacts in the period between the foundation of the Museum in 1753 and the early nineteenth century form the foundations of modern understanding of the world. Nowhere else can this topic be so fully illustrated as in the British Museum.

1 The interior of the Round Reading Room, designed by Robert Smirke's brother Sydney, has been restored and the dome regilded.

2 The Queen Elizabeth II Great Court viewed from the South Portico.

3 View of the Museum from the south-west showing the glass roof designed by Foster and Partners surrounding the dome of the Round Reading Room.

The Ancient Near East

The area known today as the ancient Near East stretches over most of the modern Middle East, covering the Gulf States, Iran, Iraq, Syria, Jordan, Israel, Lebanon and Turkey. The Syrian and Arabian deserts lie in the centre of this region, and people lived, in ancient times as now, within the so-called Fertile Crescent, where rain or rivers provide enough water to survive. The Tigris and Euphrates rivers form the south-eastern part of this crescent, a region known as Mesopotamia. The rest of the fertile zone extends north-west towards the southern coast of Turkey, also known as Anatolia. The crescent then curves south along the east coast of the Mediterranean Sea into the area known as the Levant.

The first signs of civilisation appeared within the Fertile Crescent. Around 7000BC, the Neolithic period was marked by the early domestication of animals and plants and the settling of population groups into permanent agricultural communities. Later came the manufacturing of pottery, which gradually developed into a sophisticated technology, as is demonstrated by the pot from Susa illustrated here. From the late Neolithic onwards, trade in rare goods became more widespread so that by the onset of urbanisation, materials such as lapis lazuli, obsidian and bitumen were being traded over large distances. By 3500BC, the mining, smelting and working of metals had been mastered, and it can be argued that the world's next major technological innovation did not occur until plastic was invented.

Shortly before 3000BC, the first cities emerged in Mesopotamia. Population groups became larger, and frameworks such as social stratification and craft specialisation emerged. Each city operated as a small state with its own ruler. At first, power seems to have been vested within

temples. Hence the rulers of city-states in the ancient land of Sumer, now southern Iraq, were religious figures. During this period, there was an expansion northwards in order to procure materials such as stone, wood and metal ore that were scarce in the south. The finds from the city of Tell Brak in north-east Syria show evidence for the arrival of peoples from southern Mesopotamia. The local inhabitants nevertheless maintained their customs and identity, as is shown by their distinctive 'Eye Idol' figurines.

Secular control emerged gradually within the city-states of Mesopotamia, and although religious institutions remained important, kings ruled instead

1

2

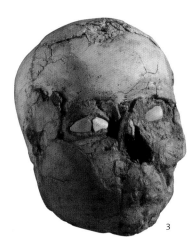

3

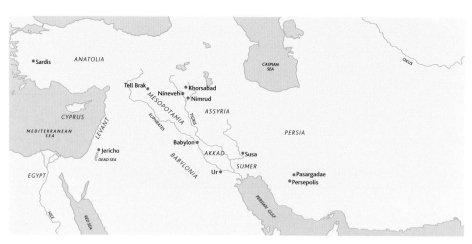

of priests. Archaeological excavations
undertaken by Sir Leonard Woolley at the
city of Ur in the 1920s uncovered magnificent burials indicating the existence of
a high-status group within the city's
population. Individuals were buried with
rich grave goods made from gold, silver,
carnelian and lapis lazuli, and were
accompanied to their graves by male
and female attendants. The largest grave
at Ur held 74 attendants, sacrificed to
accompany the main burial.

Around 2500BC, the kings of Akkad,
an area to the north of Sumer, rose to
power. Widespread military campaigns
were conducted by King Sargon and his
grandson Naram-Sin, and their power was

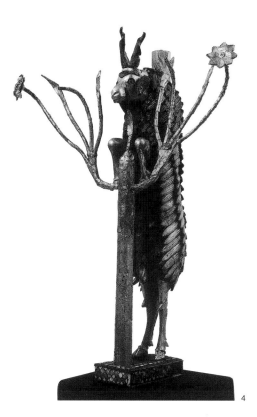

4

5

| 1 | Painted beaker. From Susa, south-west Iran, c. 4000BC.
This beautiful vessel is typical of pottery discovered in graves in a large ceme-tery at Susa. The pottery was carefully made by hand, and the finest pieces must have belonged to important people. | 2 | Alabaster 'Eye Idol'. From Tell Brak, north-eastern Syria, c. 3500–3000BC.
Hundreds of these miniature figurines with pronounced eyes have been found. They may represent worshippers and were deposited as offerings. | 3 | Plastered skull with shell-inlaid eyes. From Jericho, seventh millennium BC.
This object may have been connected with some form of ancestor cult. | 4 | The 'Ram in a Thicket'. From Ur, southern Iraq, c. 2600BC.
This is one of a pair discovered in the Royal Cemetery. Though actually a goat, it was named 'Ram in a Thicket' by Sir Leonard Woolley because he liked biblical allusions. | 5 | The 'Standard of Ur'. Shell and stone mosaic set in bitumen, originally on a wooden base, c. 2600BC.
This enigmatic object – possibly the sound-box of a musical instrument – is just one item of the vast treasure recovered by Sir Leonard Woolley from the Royal Cemetery of Ur. |

	Early Bronze Age		Late Bronze Age & Amarna period	Assyrian and Babylonian Empires
Chalcolithic		Middle Bronze Age		Iron Age
3000BC		2000BC	1000BC	

6

7

felt throughout Mesopotamia from the Gulf to the Mediterranean coast. Their influence reached as far as Tell Brak, where Naram-Sin built a fort.

In the second millennium BC, control of Mesopotamia was contested by the Assyrians from the north and Babylonians from the south. In the early first millennium, the Assyrians emerged as the dominant power and ruled Mesopotamia for 300 years from their splendid capitals at Nimrud, Khorsabad and Nineveh, now in northern Iraq. Their empire was finally overthrown by the Babylonian King Nabopolassar in 612BC. Meanwhile, other powers were emerging. From 1500BC onwards, the territory of the Hittite empire spread southwards from central Turkey through Syria until it met the border of the zone controlled by Egypt in the areas of modern Israel and Jordan. City-states in this zone traded with both Egypt and Mesopotamia and thereby accrued military and economic power. The Hittite empire collapsed around 1200BC and was superseded by smaller power bases such as the Urartians, the Phrygians and the Lydians. The Levant was controlled by the Sea Peoples and then the Phoenicians in the north and Israel and Judah further to the south, before succumbing to Assyrian rule. In Iran,

8

Assyrian and Babylonian Empires					Seleucid Era		
			Achaemenid Empire				Parthian Era
700BC	600BC	500BC	400BC	300BC	200BC	100BC	

Urartian and Assyrian invasions were
repelled by the Medes, ultimately leading
to the rise of Persia as a great power in
the sixth century BC.

Mesopotamia was the birthplace of
literacy. Initially, writing was symbolic
and designed for the keeping of accounts.
Pictograms were impressed into wet
clay using a reed as a stylus. Within this
system, an ox's head represented an ox,
and the rising sun represented a day.
Such symbols were accompanied by
circles and semi-circles that represented
numbers. By the early third millennium,
the pictograms had become highly
stylised and were no longer recognisable

10

9

6 | Mesopotamian cylinder seal (and impression). Lapis lazuli with gold caps, Akkadian period, 2333–2193BC.
Seals were rolled over damp clay tablets or the sealings of containers and doors as a form of security.

7 | Small gold figure representing a Hittite god. From Anatolia, c. 1400–1200BC.
This tiny figure is carrying a curved weapon that perhaps identifies him as a god of hunting.

8 | Ivory carving. From Nimrud, 800–750BC.
This Phoenician-style ivory, once decorated with gold leaf and inlays of lapis lazuli and carnelian, shows a Nubian boy being attacked by a lioness.

9 | Map of the world. Babylonian, c. 700–500BC, probably from Sippar, southern Iraq.
Babylon is shown in the centre of this unique map of the Mesopotamian world.

10 | Colossal statue of a winged human-headed lion from the North-West Palace of Ashurnasirpal II at Nimrud. Neo-Assyrian, c. 865BC.
This is one of a pair of guardian figures called *lamassu* set up to protect the palace from demonic forces.

Roman Empire	Byzantine Empire					
		Sasanian Empire				Arab Conquest & Islamic Era
AD100	AD200	AD300	AD400	AD500	AD600	AD700

11

Assyrian Palace Reliefs

The Neo-Assyrian kings, who controlled the Near East from Egypt to the Persian Gulf from the ninth to the seventh century BC, ruled from a series of capitals at Nimrud, Khorsabad and Nineveh. The centrepieces of these cities were the great royal palaces, with their monumental gateways protected by winged, human-headed lions and bulls and their walls lined with carved stone slabs showing royal exploits such as hunting and warfare. The British Museum is the only place where so many sequences of these magnificently preserved slabs can be seen in their original order. Excavated between 1845 and 1855, mostly by Sir Henry Layard, they include the famous reliefs of King Ashurbanipal hunting lions from his palace at Nineveh (c. 645 BC).

as pictures. Symbols developed to represent syllables, and it gradually became possible to write sentences and express ideas using 'cuneiform' wedge-shaped signs. Cuneiform became the script employed to write many of the languages used in the ancient Near East, just as the Roman alphabet is used to write a variety of languages today. A wide range of written material has been preserved on clay and stone, including letters, astrological, mathematical and historical texts, mythological tales, songs, poems, laws, decrees, maps and even a recipe for beer.

In the middle of the first millennium BC, the old powers of the Near East were overrun by Persia. It was the Medes who first extended their empire out of present-day Iran and into eastern Turkey. In turn, in the sixth century BC, the Persian King Cyrus defeated the Medes and laid claim to their territories. He constructed a grand capital at Pasargadae, captured Babylon and then established a vast empire from the Mediterranean to eastern Iran. Darius cemented this territory by crushing rebellion and establishing a system of governors called satraps. He also ordered the building of a lavish ceremonial centre at Persepolis and the 'Royal Road'

12

13

14

running thousands of miles from Susa in south-western Iran to Sardis in western Turkey.

Although the Persians held a mighty empire together, neither Darius nor his successor Xerxes managed to conquer mainland Greece, despite their repeated attempts in the fifth century BC. The splendour and wealth of the kings of Persia made their names bywords for great luxury and power among the citizens of the Greek city-states. Persia did manage to subjugate the Greek cities on the coast of western Anatolia, but these were liberated in 334BC when Alexander the Great crossed into Asia and swept into the heart of the Persian Empire. Having defeated the Persian King

Darius III in 331BC, Alexander was crowned King of Persia and married a local princess. At the height of his power, his empire stretched as far as India, but after his death it was divided between his generals.

The Near East then came under the control of the Seleucid dynasty. In 238BC, the Seleucids lost their territory east of the Euphrates to a Parthian dynasty from the north-east, and, despite the years of Greek influence, the area rapidly became hostile to western powers. Rome consequently fought several bitter campaigns against the Parthians and their successors, the Sasanians, with the region remaining under Sasanian control until the Islamic conquest in AD651.

11 The Flood Tablet. From the library of Ashurbanipal at Nineveh, seventh century BC.
Inscribed in cuneiform with the Babylonian version of the biblical story of the Flood, this tablet highlights the common ground between Semitic religions and mythologies.

12 Bronze figure of a winged bull with human torso. From Urartu, c. 700BC.

13 The Oxus Treasure. Achaemenid Persian, c. 550–400BC.
The gold bracelet with two leaping griffins and gold model of a four-horse chariot are part of a collection of precious objects allegedly discovered on the banks of the River Oxus in 1880.

14 Stone relief showing a male sphinx wearing the horned headdress of a divinity. Achaemenid Persian, fifth century BC. From Persepolis, reign of Artaxerxes III (358–338BC).
This is a Persian version of the Assyrian guardian figures (see no. 10).

The Islamic World

The history of Islam began in Arabia in AD622, when the Prophet Muhammad migrated from Mecca to Medina and established a community of believers there. Following the death of the Prophet in 632, the leadership of the Islamic community passed to a series of caliphs, the second of whom, Umar, undertook the active conversion of neighbouring lands to Islam. After the death of Umar, the Caliphate passed first to Uthman, then to Ali, the Prophet's nephew, and from him to another branch of the family, the Umayyads. The Umayyads ruled from Damascus until the mid-eighth century, when they were defeated by the Abbasids of Baghdad. By this time, the weakened Byzantine, Visigothic and Sasanian empires had succumbed to the Muslim armies, and the Islamic world stretched from Afghanistan, Iran and Iraq in the east via Syria, Egypt and the North African coast as far as Spain in the west. Great cities arose, and mosques and universities were built as centres for Islamic learning.

Many of the regions converted to Islam had venerable traditions of their own: since the mid-first millennium BC, southern Arabia had itself been the home of ancient Semitic kingdoms such as Saba, Qataban and Hadhramaut.

Far from ignoring these pre-Islamic cultures, the Arab conquerors used them to their advantage: in Syria and Iran, for example, the new Islamic regimes were openly built on the foundations of the Graeco-Roman and Sasanian cultures. This openness also extended to learning: Greek scientific and mathematical manuscripts were preserved, translated and copied by Arab and Iranian scholars, while being ignored in medieval Europe.

Nonetheless, the art of the Islamic world soon developed some common characteristics. Because the Qur'an (Koran), the Muslim holy book, is considered in Islam to be the literal word of God as revealed to Muhammad, its language, Arabic, is immutable. Thus, throughout the Muslim world Arabic was learned by educated believers. In this world bound together by the written word, calligraphy assumed the highest importance, and even the briefest texts, such as imperial monograms, were executed with the greatest attention to design. Typical of the early Islamic period, the elegant, angular Kufic script was somewhat eclipsed in later times by the flowing Naskhi and Thuluth styles. Another characteristic was the avoidance of human and animal figures in religious contexts, which encouraged the use of geometric and abstract design, including

1

Migration of the Prophet Muhammad to Medina AD622	The 'Orthodox Caliphs' AD632–661		Abbasids AD749–1258 Baghdad				
Death of Muhammad AD632	Umayyads AD661–750			Fatimids AD969–1171 Cairo			Il-Khanids 1220–c.133
AD600	AD700	AD800	AD900	AD1000	AD1100	AD1200	AD130

2

3

4

1 Brass ewer inlaid with silver. From Herat, Afghanistan, c. AD1200.

The high degree of skill achieved by Islamic metalworkers can be seen in the inlaid decoration and the relief figures of birds and lions.

2 Carved marble panel from a cenotaph. From Cairo, AD967.

Strict Islamic observance forbids the construction of elaborate tombs, so the deceased were often commemorated with cenotaphs instead. The majestic Kufic inscription reads 'In the Name of God the Merciful'.

3 Ceramic bowl. Iran. Signed by Abu Zayd. Dated Muharram AH583/March–April AD1187.

This bowl is one of five pieces produced by the master potter Abu Zayd in Muharram, the first month of the Muslim year. The decorative technique, called mina'i, requires two firings in which some colours are applied over the transparent glaze and some under it.

4 Gold dinar of the Abbasid Caliph al-Musta'sim, AD1242–58.

There are many different ways of ornamenting Kufic script. The ends of the letters on this coin are extended as foliage.

Mamluks AD1250–1517 Cairo		Mughals AD1526–1858 Delhi, Agra				
	AD1453 Ottomans conquer Istanbul		Ottomans c. AD1281–1924			
	Timurids 1370–1506	Safavids AD1501–1722 Iran		Qajars AD1779–1925		
AD1400	AD1500	AD1600	AD1700	AD1800	AD1900	AD2000

the graceful stylised plant motifs known as arabesques.

Even during the lifetime of the Prophet Muhammad, decorative arts – textiles, ceramics, glass and metal objects – were noted for the beauty of their workmanship. They continued to play a significant role in the Islamic world and were natural vehicles for the decorative vocabulary that characterises Islamic art. Thus geometric designs, arabesques in the form of vine scrolls, and calligraphy appear alone or combined on the range of Islamic decorative arts. Animal and human imagery also adorns portable objects used in secular settings as well as non-religious architecture from early Islamic times onward. From the ninth century, trade with the East introduced Chinese silks and porcelains, which were to have a profound effect on textile and ceramic design and technology. Although Muslim potters lacked the materials and kilns necessary to produce porcelain, their efforts to duplicate its whiteness and translucence led to new glazing techniques and ultimately the eleventh-century development of a hard, white ceramic material called stonepaste. With this new ware, potters from Egypt, Syria and Iran produced ceramics in a dazzling array of shapes, colours and glaze types. Likewise, from the second half of the twelfth century onwards metalworkers in the eastern Muslim world adopted the new technique of inlaying brass objects with copper, gold and silver. Ideas introduced through trade with Europe led, for example, to the Venetian enamelled-glass industry and encouraged the use of precious-metal inlays on brass vessels.

The second half of the millennium saw the establishment of larger empires and more enduring dynasties. Among them were the Ottomans, conquerors of the eastern Byzantine territories and the Mamluk empire, who made Istanbul their capital in 1453; the Safavids, who ruled Iran from the sixteenth to the eighteenth century; their successors, the Qajars, who lasted into the twentieth century; and the Mughals, who controlled much of India between the sixteenth and nineteenth centuries.

5

6

7

The Islamic Faith

Muslims believe that the faith of Islam – which means 'submission' – was divinely revealed to the Prophet Muhammad, who had it set down in the holy book, known as the Qu'ran. They believe in one God and acknowledge the Old Testament prophets and Jesus, though as another prophet, not as the Son of God. There is no priesthood in Islam, although there are religious scholars who give legal and theological opinions, and most mosques have an imam to lead prayers. All Muslims must observe the 'Five Pillars' of Islam. The first of these is the affirmation that there is only one God and that the Prophet Muhammad is the Messenger of God. The second is prayer. The third is almsgiving, the fourth is fasting during the holy month of Ramadan, and the fifth is the making, if possible, of the Pilgrimage to Mecca.

8

9

5 Spherical incense burner. Made for Badr al-Din Baysari. Brass inlaid with silver. Syria, 1277–9.

The owner of this incense burner was a wealthy and powerful minister at the Mamluk court. Fixed with a saucer for incense suspended from metal rings inside it, this sphere typifies the opulent inlaid brasses of Mamluk Egypt and Syria.

6 Glass mosque lamp. From Egypt or Syria, AD1330–35.

The Mamluk sultans ruled Egypt and Syria from the mid-thirteenth to the early sixteenth century, and large numbers of enamelled and gilded glass lamps were commissioned for the many mosques they and their court officials built in Cairo.

7 Brass astrolabe. From Iran, AD1712.

The astrolabe was especially important in Muslim society as it was used to give the times and direction of prayer (performed five times a day while facing Mecca). This magnificent example was made for the Safavid ruler Shah Sultan Husayn.

8 Ceramic basin. From Iznik, Turkey, AD1530–40.

Made in the famous Iznik potteries, this large footed basin is elaborately decorated with swirling blossoms and leaves painted in underglaze purple, green, blue and black.

9 Dagger with gold hilt and chape set with rubies and emeralds. Mughal India, c. 1625.

The Mughal emperors were renowned collectors of gems and jewelled items like this dagger, set with rubies in the shape of foxes, lions and deer. The gold is worked in a style associated with the court workshop of Jahangir in the 1620s.

Africa

The African continent has provided archaeologists with some of the earliest evidence of human activities. Stone working began just over 2,000,000 years ago, and long stretches of its development can be observed at Olduvai Gorge in Tanzania, where large hand axes were among the earliest stone tools produced. Although these could be quite versatile, a major breakthrough came about 120,000 years ago with a technological development that enabled the manufacture of smaller, more precise flint blades – ranging from sizeable spearheads to tiny 'microliths' – which could be fitted to shafts of wood, bone or antler to create useful tools for hunting and gathering food. Engraved pieces of red ochre recently discovered in South Africa have been dated to about 70,000 years ago, indicating the very early emergence of modern human behaviour.

Conditions in the fertile Nile Valley led to the gradual domestication of animals and the development of agriculture over many thousands of years. Around 3100BC, the lower Nile Valley and Delta were consolidated to form the kingdom of Egypt, which remained dominant in the region for several millennia. Artistic expression reached great levels of sophistication, with the construction of elaborate tombs and temples and the production of fine sculptures, wall paintings, ceramics and jewellery.

The relationship between Egypt and its southern neighbours was volatile. Nubia, more particularly the kingdom of Kush, whose capital was at Kerma, played a vital role in supplying Egypt with gold and with African luxury goods such as ivory, ebony, incense and exotic animal skins. However, although Egypt controlled the region intermittently, Kush was itself a strong and organised society, and in the eighth century BC the tables were turned when a powerful Kushite dynasty from Napata succeeded in conquering Egypt, establishing the Twenty-fifth Dynasty.

Although its rule in Egypt lasted less than a century, Kush, with its capital of Meroë, remained a major power for another thousand years. Like its predecessors, the Kushite kingdom thrived on trade and war, on one occasion causing grave problems for the Romans, who colonised much of North Africa between the second and first centuries BC. The art of Meroë

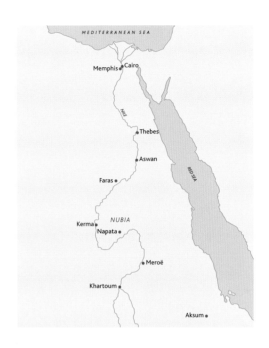

2

1

TIMELINE OF ARCHAEOLOGICAL PERIODS OF THE NILE VALLEY				'A Group' – A Horizon 3500–2800BC		
5000BC	4500BC	4000BC	3500BC	3000BC	2500BC	2000

was heavily influenced by that of Egypt and Rome, and Kushite royalty were buried in tombs beneath pyramids. In the third century AD, however, Kush was eclipsed by the Christian state of Aksum in northern Ethiopia, which became the main route for trade between central Africa and the Mediterranean.

The latter part of the first millennium AD saw the loosening of links between northern and sub-Saharan Africa; as the desert expanded, contact was increasingly restricted to coastal regions and the trans-Saharan caravans. North Africa embraced first Christianity, then Islam, leading to the establishment of great cities such as Cairo in Egypt, Fes in Morocco and Kairouan in Tunisia. By the tenth century, Islam had begun to spread into West Africa, becoming the main religion among the great empires of Tekrur, Ghana, Songhay and Mali, where Timbuktu became a noted centre of Islamic scholarship.

By the beginning of the second millennium AD, prosperous Muslim communities were becoming established along the East African coast, trading with powerful kingdoms inland and laying the foundations of the Swahili culture. In all of these areas, Islamic strictures against representational art led to a focus on architectural decoration, leatherwork and

1 | Pottery bowls. From Faras, 'C Group'.
Pottery was produced in the Nile Valley from Neolithic times onwards. These polished and incised wares typify the local style of Lower Nubia.

2 | 'Tulip' beaker. From Kush, c. 1750–1550BC.
This hand-formed beaker was found in a tomb alongside other artefacts intended to assist the deceased in the afterlife.

3 | Sphinx of Tarharqo from a temple in Kawa, Nubia. Twenty-fifth Dynasty, c. 680BC.
The lion's mane was inspired by earlier Egyptian sphinxes, but the double uraeus, the skull cap and the face are purely Nubian in style.

4 | Wall painting. From Thebes, Egypt, New Kingdom, c. 1400BC.
This painting from a tomb chapel shows Nubians presenting African products – including gold, incense and animal skins – to the Egyptian Pharaoh.

Group' – C Horizon 00–1500BC	New Kingdom – Egyptian occupation 1550–1069BC	Napatan Period 1000–300BC	Meroitic Period 300BC–AD350	Christian Period AD550–1500	
rma 00–1500BC		25th Dynasty, Nubian rule over Egypt c. 747–656BC		Ballana Culture (X Group), Noba AD350–550	Islamic Period AD1500–
1500BC	1000BC	500BC	0	AD500	AD1000	AD1500

5

textiles. In the non-Muslim kingdoms of West Africa, certain valuable objects and materials – especially metals – were the prerogative of kings and chiefs. Indeed, the institution of kingship, which dates from the early second millennium AD, was closely connected with the production and control of metals. In Ghana, for example, the kings and chiefs of the Asante people once controlled the local gold trade as a means of obtaining firearms from European traders. They still make extensive use of local gold in their elaborate regalia, while miniature brass sculptures of humans and animals are used as weights for measuring gold dust. In Nigeria, craftsmen attached to the courts of Benin and Ife produced finely detailed cast bronzes and ivory carvings. In some cases, the supernatural powers of a ruler were considered to render him potentially dangerous to his subjects; thus royal and divine imagery is often closely connected.

Such religious thinking played an important role in African material culture generally, and especially in the art of the peoples inhabiting the dense forest regions stretching along the southern coast of West Africa to the Congo basin. The close proximity and complex histories of these communities resulted in a wide variety of local styles, often used as markers of ethnic identity and affiliation. Prolific wood-carvers, these peoples mainly produced religious images and masks, which play an important ritual role in many parts of Africa and are regarded as objects of great power. Other arts, such as smithing and pottery, had a greater significance in areas without strong traditions of figurative wood-carving.

In the forests and savannahs of central Africa, wood carvers tended to produce more decorative items such as cups, furniture and boxes, although the Kuba of the Democratic Republic of Congo are also

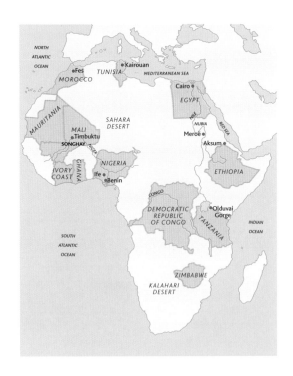

6

7

5 Sandstone carving. From Faras, seventh century AD.
   Part of a frieze from the first Christian cathedral at Faras, showing a cross above a bird's head.

6 Cast brass head. Benin, Nigeria, *c.* fifteenth century AD.
   Copper and its alloys were considered a royal material in Benin. Heads like this were cast after the deaths of kings exclusively for the altars of Benin City, being commissioned by heirs to the throne.

7 Wood mask. Guro people, Ivory Coast, nineteenth/twentieth century AD.
   Many African masquerades harness the powers of the spirit world for the wellbeing of the people. This mask appears to mix animal and human attributes and is associated with bush spirits.

8

9

10

noted for their masks and the fine sculpted figures of their kings. Elsewhere in eastern and southern Africa, there is a more apparent emphasis on body decoration, though the Masai, Zulu and Shona peoples also take pride in their elaborate shields and weapons. Parts of South Africa and the Sahara are famous for their sites containing painted rock surfaces, a tradition preserved from antiquity to the present day.

The first direct documented contacts between European traders and sub-Saharan Africa occurred in the fifteenth century. In later centuries, European colonisation and the forced deportation of thousands of Africans as slaves were to have a profound effect on the development of American, Caribbean and British culture. Just as early twentieth-century African art provided inspiration to European painters and sculptors, so contemporary African artists are adopting and adapting European art forms to develop new expressions of their traditions. The work of many contemporary artists, created both within and outside the continent, echoes the dynamism and continuing significance of ancient African traditions. It also helps towards an understanding of ways in which perceptions of Africa and African art are changing in the globalising world of the 21st century. These works and the multiple identities of many of their creators do not suggest some sort of distillation of 'Africanness'. Instead, they emphasise the extraordinary cultural, ethnic, geographical, artistic and historical diversity of Africa, as well as the continent's immense impact on the rest of the world.

11

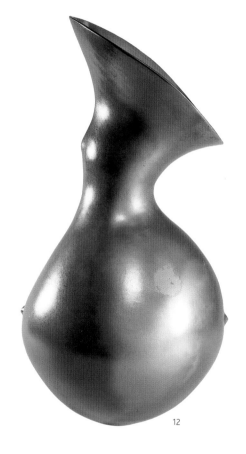

12

8 Copper and iron throwing knives. Nzakara people, Central African Republic, nineteenth century AD.

Although they do not seem to have played a significant part in traditional warfare, throwing knives were highly personal male accessories, often beautifully forged and described in terms of the human image.

9 Appliqué banner, possibly made by Acheampong. Fante people, Ghana, nineteenth century AD.

Historically, such banners represented individual *asafo* (war people), militia groups which, for centuries, brokered the balance of power between Europeans on the coast and African kingdoms inland. They are still produced today.

10 Soapstone figurine. Zimbabwe, *c.* thirteenth century AD.

The Shona kingdom of Great Zimbabwe rose to power in the 1200s. Among the various stone carvings attributed to the Zimbabwe culture are these anthropomorphic figurines, variously interpreted as votive offerings, symbols of a fertility complex and royal regalia.

11 Wool and cotton textile. Peul people, Niger, twentieth century AD.

Though woven in the distinctively West African technique of narrow-strip, the patterning of this cloth is essentially of North African (Berber) inspiration. It reflects the ancient pattern of trade via the trans-Saharan caravan routes.

12 Ceramic vessel by Magdalene Odundo, Farnham, UK, 2000.

Born in Kenya, but based in the UK, Odundo shares a concern with the exploration of form by artists across the ages, both within and outside Africa.

Egypt

In the sixth millennium BC, the people of the Nile Valley began to take a different cultural path from the rest of Africa. Already skilled hunters and stone workers, they began to turn their attention to the cultivation of the rich Nile silt. The establishment of settled communities led to the development of simple industries such as pottery making and copper smelting. By around 3600BC, these Predynastic Egyptians were hunting with sophisticated flint weapons, producing painted pottery and building shrines of reeds and mud to the local deities who were later to make up the complex Egyptian pantheon. The earliest Egyptian writing appeared, rapidly developing into the largely phonetic hieroglyphic script. The names of individual kings began to be recorded, including those of Narmer and Aha. Egyptian tradition records that a southern ruler gained control of the whole country around 3100BC and established the first national capital at Memphis, close to the junction of the Nile Valley and Delta.

This symbolic unification of the 'Two Lands' of Upper Egypt (the Valley) and Lower Egypt (the Delta) was central to Egyptian ideas of kingship. Known as 'Pharaoh', meaning 'Great House', the King was regarded as both human and divine. In life, he was seen as the son of the sun-god Ra and the human incarnation of the falcon-god Horus; in death, as Osiris, the Lord of the Underworld. Temples to the gods were exploited as vehicles for royal propaganda, incorporating huge statues and relief carvings of the King in traditional attitudes as the unifier and defender of Egypt.

Long king-lists carved on temple walls were tailored to political expediency; discredited kings – and all female rulers – were simply removed from the official record. No attempt at writing history in the modern sense is known to have been made until around 250BC, when a priest called Manetho compiled a list of 30 dynasties, or ruling families. Modern historians grouped these into 'Kingdoms' – periods of relative stability – separated

1

2

Predynastic 5500–3100BC		Old Kingdom c. 2686–2181BC		Middle Kingdom c. 2055–1650BC	
	Early Dynastic c. 3100–2686BC		1st Intermediate c. 2181–2055BC		2nd Intermediate c. 1650–155●
	3000BC	2500BC		2000BC	

3

by 'Intermediate Periods' characterised by war or political fragmentation.

Despite the impression of continuity given by the use of traditional imagery in official art, cultural and political alignments often changed, as is indicated by the frequent shifts of administrative centre as dynasties from different localities came to power. These often reflected the ancient rivalry between the north and the south: Thebes in Upper Egypt enjoyed prominence for extended periods during the Middle and New Kingdoms, but was eventually superseded by a series of Delta cities including Tanis.

4

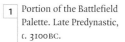 Portion of the Battlefield Palette. Late Predynastic, c. 3100BC.

Cosmetic palettes were used for preparing eyepaint to protect against infections. Decorated examples like this had a ceremonial function in Egypt's earliest temples.

2 The Pitt-Rivers Knife. Predynastic, c. 3600–3250BC.

The finely worked flint blade is fitted with an ivory handle carved with figures of animals.

3 Part of a king-list from the temple of Ramesses II at Abydos. New Kingdom, c. 1250BC.

The hieroglyphs in the oval enclosures, or cartouches, spell out the name of Ramesses II and those of previous pharaohs.

4 Upper part of a colossal statue of the Nineteenth-Dynasty Pharaoh Ramesses II, from his memorial temple at Thebes. New Kingdom, c. 1270BC.

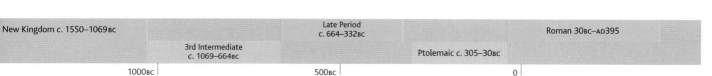

New Kingdom c. 1550–1069BC		Late Period c. 664–332BC		Roman 30BC–AD395
	3rd Intermediate c. 1069–664BC		Ptolemaic c. 305–30BC	
1000BC		500BC		0

Dynasties of Egypt

EARLY DYNASTIC PERIOD
First Dynasty c. 3100–2890BC
Second Dynasty c. 2890–2686BC

OLD KINGDOM
Third Dynasty c. 2686–2613BC
Fourth Dynasty c. 2613–2494BC
Fifth Dynasty c. 2494–2345BC
Sixth Dynasty c. 2345–2181BC

FIRST INTERMEDIATE PERIOD
Seventh/Eighth Dynasty c. 2181–2125BC
Ninth/Tenth Dynasty
c. 2160–2130BC, c. 2125–2025BC
Eleventh Dynasty (Thebes only)
c. 2125–2055BC

MIDDLE KINGDOM
Eleventh Dynasty (all Egypt)
c. 2055–1985BC
Twelfth Dynasty c. 1985–1795BC
Thirteenth Dynasty c. 1795–1650BC
Fourteenth Dynasty c. 1750–1650BC

SECOND INTERMEDIATE PERIOD
Fifteenth Dynasty (Hyksos) c. 1650–1550BC
Sixteenth Dynasty c. 1650–1550BC
Seventeenth Dynasty c. 1650–1550BC

NEW KINGDOM
Eighteenth Dynasty c. 1550–1295BC
Nineteenth Dynasty c. 1295–1186BC
Twentieth Dynasty c. 1186–1069BC

THIRD INTERMEDIATE PERIOD
Twenty-first Dynasty c. 1069–945BC
Twenty-second Dynasty c. 945–715BC
Twenty-third Dynasty c. 818–715BC
Twenty-fourth Dynasty c. 727–715BC
Twenty-fifth Dynasty (Nubian or Kushite)
c. 747–656BC

LATE PERIOD
Twenty-sixth Dynasty (Saite) 664–525BC
Twenty-seventh Dynasty (Persian kings)
525–404BC
Twenty-eighth Dynasty 404–399BC
Twenty-ninth Dynasty 399–380BC
Thirtieth Dynasty 380–343BC
Persian kings 343–332BC

GRECO-ROMAN PERIOD
Macedonian kings 332–305BC
Ptolemies 305–30BC
Roman emperors 30BC–AD395

5

Mummification

Egyptian cemeteries were commonly sited in the desert to the west of towns and cities. The earliest burials were made directly into pits in the ground, where they were preserved by the hot, dry sand. A belief in life after death was current by Predynastic times, when burials typically included simple grave goods. For the well-to-do, the Egyptians started to construct veritable tombs of mud-brick and, later, stone. To preserve the body as a home for the ka – the deceased's life force – the practice of mummification was developed. After the removal of the internal organs – which were separately preserved in four containers known as canopic jars – the body was dried out using natron, a natural salt. Finally, it was wrapped in linen bandages and placed in a coffin. As incarnate gods, the pharaohs underwent especially elaborate mummification. They were carefully bandaged with fine linen, their bodies covered with protective amulets and jewellery. A gold mask was placed over the neck and head before the royal mummy was encased in a series of coffins and placed in a huge stone sarcophagus in the burial chamber.

7

During the Third Intermediate Period Egypt first came under Nubian rule, then in the Late Period suffered repeated attack from emerging foreign powers such as the Assyrians and Persians. The second Persian conquest in 343BC brought native Egyptian rule to a definitive end, and in 332BC Alexander the Great claimed Egypt as part of his empire. Following Alexander's death, his general Ptolemy established his own dynasty. With a new capital at Alexandria on the northern coast, Egypt became increasingly involved in the cultural and political world of the Greek Mediterranean; this process intensified after 30BC, when the last Ptolemaic ruler, Cleopatra VII, was defeated by Octavian, and Egypt became a part of the Roman Empire.

Although the Persian, Greek and Roman rulers had themselves represented in conventional pharaonic attitudes and found it expedient to support and build temples, they were less concerned with Egypt's religion and culture than its legendary wealth. At the height of its power during the New Kingdom, Egypt's empire had extended south to the fourth Nile cataract in Nubia and as far north as the modern-day border between Syria

5 Head of a colossal red granite statue of Amenophis III. From Karnak, Eighteenth Dynasty, c. 1390BC.
The crowned head is nearly 3 metres high.

6 Gilded inner coffin of Henutmehyt, a priestess of the god Amun during the reign of Ramesses II. Nineteenth Dynasty, c. 1250BC.

7 Mummy of the Twenty-Second-Dynasty priestess Tjentmutengebtiu, c. 900BC.
The coffin is painted with protective images and deities.

6

8

9

and Turkey. As well as controlling the trade in exotic goods from Africa – ebony, ivory and gold – Egypt produced such desirable export goods as linen, papyrus and grain – grain that Rome in particular needed to feed its expanding empire.

Much of what we know about the ancient Egyptians derives from their tombs and the artefacts placed in them for their owners to enjoy in the afterlife.

From the Early Dynastic period, mastaba tombs modelled on the homes of the living were constructed for the élite at such sites as Abydos in the south and Saqqara in the north. In the Old and Middle Kingdoms, pharaohs were buried in enormous pyramid complexes like those at Giza, but from the New Kingdom onwards, they preferred the greater security of tombs cut into the ground or hillside, as in the Valley of the Kings at Thebes or the temple precinct at Tanis.

Paintings and reliefs inside the tombs illustrate the complex funerary beliefs

10

11

12

8 Wall painting from the tomb of Nebamun, an Eighteenth-Dynasty Theban official. New Kingdom, c. 1390BC.

The scene represents a banquet, with musicians and dancers.

9 Funerary model of a man ploughing with oxen. Early Middle Kingdom, c. 1950BC.

Models of servants at work were included in burials to ensure a regular supply of foodstuffs for the tomb owner.

10 Painted wooden box containing *shabtis* made for the Nineteenth-Dynasty Theban priestess Henutmehyt.

Shabtis were magical figurines placed in the tomb to work on behalf of the deceased in the next world.

11 Another wall painting from the tomb of Nebamun, who is represented fowling in the marshes with a throw-stick, accompanied by his wife, daughter and cat. The scene is charged with erotic symbolism and evokes the triumph of order over chaos.

12 Papyrus 'Book of the Dead' written for the Nineteenth-Dynasty royal scribe Any. New Kingdom, c. 1250BC.

'Books of the Dead', known to the Egyptians as the 'Chapters of Coming Forth by Day', were collections of magic spells and instructions intended to guide and protect the deceased in the afterlife.

13

14

of the ancient Egyptians; however, it was only with the decipherment of the accompanying texts in the nineteenth century that these began to be under-stood. Royal tomb paintings often depict the strange geography and terrifying creatures of the Underworld, through which the sun-god travelled at night. After death, the soul followed the sun through the underworld and entered the court of the god Osiris. Here, the deceased's heart was weighed to ascertain its righteousness; if it passed the test, the soul would achieve a peaceful afterlife on the god's estates.

In many periods, the tombs of wealthy commoners were carved and painted with vivid scenes of everyday life. These were

not just meant for decoration; like all Egyptian funerary art, their purpose was in part to provide the deceased magically with everything required for the afterlife. Representations of officials supervising agricultural activities or enjoying family parties, for example, were created to allow them to continue their earthly status and pleasures in the next world. Other commonly included scenes show the owner's funeral and the bringing of offerings by relatives, subordinates and priests to sustain his *ka* (or life-force) after death. In addition, tombs were stocked with all the necessities of life – food, clothing, cosmetics, jewellery, writing materials and furniture; often

preserved intact by Egypt's dry climate, these provide valuable information about the details of ancient life. Specifically funerary objects included models of boats, animals and servants, as well as amulets to protect the body. Papyrus scrolls with extracts from the 'Book of the Dead' provided spells to help the dead in the afterlife.

Very little material survives outside tombs and temples, but some sites have provided objects straight from daily life, as well as a mass of texts ranging from laundry lists to letters and literary compositions.

Egyptian Gods and their Cults

The Egyptian religion was a system of ancient cults based around the natural cycles on which Egypt's agricultural economy depended. Deities personifying these natural forces were often worshipped in local 'triads' comprising a god, his spouse and their child, for example Ptah, Sekhmet and Nefertum at Memphis, Osiris, Isis and Horus at Abydos and Amun, Mut and Khons at Thebes. Some gods, such as Ptah or Osiris, were always shown as humans, but many others took the form or the head of animals, such as the falcon Horus or the lioness Sekhmet. These animals eventually came to be regarded as actual manifestations of the gods, and in the Late and Graeco-Roman periods they were often mummified. As intermediary between the gods and humanity, the pharaoh was responsible for maintaining earthly and cosmic order, and vast temples were dedicated to the gods in order to enlist their support.

15

16

17

---

13 Figure of the domestic god Bes playing a tambourine. From Akhmim, New Kingdom, c. 1550–1069 BC.
   The fierce-looking Bes was believed to ward off bad spirits from pregnant women and the household.

14 Blue faience *shabti* figure of Pharaoh Sety I from his tomb in the Valley of the Kings at Thebes. New Kingdom, c. 1280 BC.
   The inscribed '*shabti* spell' asserts that, should the owner be commanded to do any labour in the hereafter, the *shabti* would do it in his stead.

15 Evidence of the Late Period animal cults. The bronze Gayer Anderson Cat, from after 600 BC, represents the goddess Bastet; a silvered pectoral bears the sacred eye of Horus. The intricately wrapped mummy of a cat is from Abydos, Roman Period, after 30 BC.

16 Glazed composition amulet comprising the hieroglyphs for 'life, stability and power'. Late Period, c. 700–500 BC.

17 Glazed composition hippopotamus decorated with aquatic plants. Middle Kingdom, c. 1900 BC.

China

Rice, a staple food in China, was being cultivated along the fertile south-east coast by 5000BC. Settled societies grew, developing distinctive traits expressed in jade-carving and in the production of ritual and decorative ceramics.

Later tradition dated the earliest ruling dynasty, the Xia, to the period around 2000BC, but the first dynasty for which there is archaeological evidence is the Shang, which came to power around 1500BC. The large, well-defined Shang capitals in the Yellow River valley were equipped with palaces and temples and surrounded by rich burial sites. The use of bronze for weaponry, ornaments and ritual objects was of central importance to the Shang and their successors. During the Shang and Western Zhou periods, great numbers of bronze vessels and weapons were buried in tombs and hoards, while valuable artefacts were dedicated to ancestors in the hope of their assistance or in gratitude for services performed.

The Shang period also saw the earliest use of writing in the form of inscribed oracle bones and shells. This system was to prove one of the most important instruments in creating a unified Chinese cultural tradition; even today, many of the

1

2

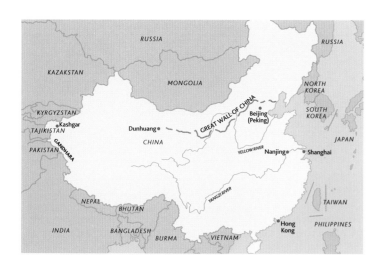

3

Neolithic (to 1500BC)	Shang (c. 1500–1050BC)		Western Zhou (1050–771BC)					
						Eastern Zhou (770–221BC) Spring and Autumn period (770–475BC)		
1200BC	1100BC	1000BC	900BC	800BC	700BC	600BC	500	

ancient characters remain in use. Under the Eastern Zhou (770–221BC), ink and bamboo were used to record rituals, political proceedings, history and philosophy, marking the beginning of the Chinese literary tradition.

In 221BC, following a period of violent civil discord and interstate rivalry, Qin Shi Huangdi succeeded in uniting the whole of China, ushering in the imperial period. Although the dynasty he founded was short-lived, the Qin government left a lasting legacy in the form of a reformed writing system, a network of roads, a unified coinage and a standardised system of weights and measures. The Qin also made one of the first attempts to construct a 'Great Wall' in the north; intended to exclude the nomad tribes of the steppes beyond, this long border defence was created by linking short sections of wall built by previous regimes.

The Qin were overthrown by the Han dynasty (206BC–AD220), whose reign continued the development of the bureaucracy so characteristic of imperial China. Men were largely recruited for government service on the basis of personal recommendation, but military skill and literary ability were the qualities which helped individuals to advance. In the early empire, guidance on the conduct of government was provided by two widely diverging philosophies,

4

| 1 | Carvings in jade and other hard stones. Neolithic, c. 3500 BC.

Jades such as these are thought to have been made for ceremonial purposes and to have a protective function, warding off evil spirits both in life and after death.

| 2 | Bronze ritual vessel. Early–middle Western Zhou period (1050–771 BC).

This inscribed vessel was cast for the Duke of Xing, a descendant of the famous Duke of Zhou. Large bronzes tended to be used for ritual and ceremonial purposes and have been excavated in vast quantities from various burial sites.

| 3 | Silver comb with repoussé decoration of birds and flowers, enhanced with gilding. Tang/Liao dynasty, c. AD618–1125.

Hair ornaments and buckles were two of the main forms of personal adornment in China.

| 4 | Wooden guardian figure crowned by antlers made of dry lacquer. Eastern Zhou period, 4th–3rd century BC.

Wooden figures with monstrous faces, long tongues and antlers were placed as guardians in Chu tombs in southern Henan and northern Hubei provinces. This example is one of very few such artefacts surviving today.

				Southern and Northern dynasties (AD265–581)
		Qin 221–207BC		Three Kingdoms (AD221–280)
Warring States (475–221BC)		Western Han (206BC–AD9)	Xin (AD9–25)	Eastern Han (AD25–220)
400BC	300BC	200BC	100BC	0	AD100	AD200

5

Confucianism and Daoism. Confucius
(551–479BC) was a philosopher and
teacher of political conduct whose
doctrines emphasised moral order, the
strict observance of ritual and tradition,
and the cultivation of the civilised arts.
Daoism, on the other hand, advocated
the 'Way of Heaven', a path of harmony
with nature and the cosmos. Best
known through the works of Lao Zi
(c. 604–531BC), the ultimate goal of
Daoism is immortality, attained through
control of the mind and attunement
to the infinite.

Following the collapse of the Han
dynasty, the north underwent a period
of fragmentation and foreign rule. This
political decentralisation coincided with
the spread of Buddhism, brought to
China by Indian monks via the Silk Route,
the great trade route connecting South
Asia and China with the Mediterranean
world via the oases of Central Asia.
Important centres of art and trade developed at Kashgar and Dunhuang, where
the artistic influences of Gandhara and
Kashmir can be seen in rock-cut monas-
teries and stupas, wall paintings and

Southern and Northern dynasties (AD265–581)		Tang (AD618–906)			Liao (AD907–1125)		
							Jin (AD1115–1234
	Sui (AD589–618)				Five Dynasties (AD907–960)	Northern Song (AD960–1126)	Southern Song (AD1127–1279)
AD500	AD600	AD700	AD800	AD900	AD1000	AD1100	AD12

religious sculptures. Central Asian art in turn exerted a profound influence on the Buddhist art of northern China between the fourth and sixth centuries AD.

In AD589, China was reunified under the Sui dynasty, whose rulers patronised Buddhism as a state religion. They in turn were followed by the Tang (AD618–906), whose magnificent court was famous as a centre of the arts. The importance of trade along the Silk Route in this period is reflected in the glazed earthenware models of horses and camels, as well as silver vessels, that have survived.

During the Song dynasty (AD960–1279), control of the north became difficult to maintain due to constant foreign incursions; eventually, in 1127, a Jurchen invasion from the north-east forced the Song rulers to retreat southwards.

6

7

8

5 Painted clay, wood and silk funerary model of a horse. Turfan, Xinjiang province, western China, Tang dynasty, eighth century AD.

This figure was made for the tomb of a high-ranking ruler or merchant living in Gaochang. Funerary sculptures of this type were fabricated as replicas of the glazed tomb models made in metropolitan areas.

6 Two cast bronze semi-naked wrestling figures. Possibly from South China, Eastern Zhou dynasty, fifth–fourth century BC.

Apart from tomb figurines, human sculpture was rare in China before the arrival of Buddhism from India. These may have been a support-vessel. Wrestling acrobats were popular entertainers in China.

7 White fine stoneware ewer in the form of a mermaid with wings. North China, Liao dynasty, AD907–1125.

Porcelain and fine white stonewares were being made at a number of kilns in China by the tenth century. This object may have been made as a substitute for silver wares for burial, for Buddhist ritual usc, or as an amusing serving vessel for wine.

8 Red carved-lacquer ingot-shaped dish showing dragons and the Eighteen Luohan. Ming dynasty, Jiajing mark and period, AD1522–66.

Lacquer is a luxury item that is extremely labour-intensive to produce. Each of the Eighteen Luohan is shown with their own attribute, including the Tiger Tamer and Bodhidharma floating on a reed.

						People's Republic (AD1949–)
	Ming (AD1368–1644)					
Yuan (AD1279–1368)				Qing (AD1644–1911)		Republic (AD1912–1949)
AD1300	AD1400	AD1500	AD1600	AD1700	AD1800	AD1900

9

Henceforth, the capital of north China was sited at Beijing, and it was here that the Mongols later established their capital, Khambaliq, from which they ruled the whole of China. Despite the northern threat, the Southern Song period was one of intense intellectual and cultural activity, much of it directed towards understanding Chinese history and the role of the state. Confucian thought underwent a revival, and new editions of the Confucian canon were published, taking advantage of the newly developed technology of printing.

A huge market existed for printed editions of the Buddhist scriptures, since they formed the syllabus of a state-run examination system that had originated and developed during the Sui and Tang dynasties. The Song interest in tradition had its counterpart in the decorative arts. The influence of early jades and bronzes, for example, can be seen in the heavy, rounded shape of Song stonewares, while fine Song porcelains often mimic the elegant forms of beaten gold and silver vessels.

With the end of Mongol rule in the fourteenth century, imperial power passed to another native dynasty, the Ming

10

(1368–1644), who established their capital at Nanjing for a brief period before moving it back to Beijing. Building on techniques developed by Yuan artisans, Ming artists produced porcelains painted with underglaze blue or overglaze enamel colours, spectacular carved lacquer wares, cloisonné enamels and gilt-bronze sculptures.

In 1644, Manchurian invaders from the north ousted the Ming, establishing the last imperial dynasty, the Qing, who ruled until 1911. As in earlier times, Qing art reflected a respect for the past, favouring traditional forms and techniques. There were also numerous innovations, however, especially in the decorative arts, notably the *famille verte* and *famille rose* enamel palettes.

11

12

9 Porcelain dish painted with a fish among water plants. Yuan dynasty, fourteenth century AD.

Overseas trade boomed during the Yuan dynasty. Among the imports from Iran was cobalt. Its use in the first quarter of the 1300s on the high-quality white porcelain from Jingdezhen had a fundamental impact on ceramics throughout the world.

10 Stoneware figure from a judgement group. Ming dynasty, sixteenth century AD.

The belief in hell entered China with Buddhism during the early first millennium AD. From the late Tang dynasty onwards, such statues depicting characters from the underworld were common.

11 Large cloisonné jar. Ming dynasty, Xuande mark and period, 1426–35.

Cloisonné enamel vessels were used by the imperial court for palaces and temples where their bright colours were shown to advantage, but were considered vulgar by the scholarly class.

12 Hell money, twentieth century AD.

It is traditional to burn imitation bank notes printed in the name of the Bank of Hell as offerings to the ancestors in the spirit world.

South & South-East Asia

The oldest human settlements in South Asia date to the eighth millennium BC, but it was not until the third millennium that a complex urban civilisation developed in and around the Indus Valley. Harappa, Mohenjo-Daro, Lothal and other sites were large, planned cities suggestive of an ordered and centralised society. Steatite seals carved with undeciphered inscriptions survive in considerable numbers and seem to have been used for commercial purposes.

From approximately 1900BC, the Indus civilisation declined. Nomadic peoples from Central Asia began to enter the subcontinent, among them tribal groups speaking Indo-European languages. With their horses and chariots, these people pushed rapidly across north India. By 900BC they were settling in villages, mixing with local populations. This was the age of philosophical and religious enquiry from which the complex Hindu religion emerged.

From approximately 500BC a new process of urbanisation began. The largest

1

centres included Hastinapura, Kausambi, Varanasi and Pataliputra in the Gangetic plain. The Buddha lived at this time. Directly opposed to all forms of violence, he specifically attacked the efficacy of sacrifice, a cornerstone of the orthodox social order. The contemporaneous growth in population was due to improvements in land management and food production, particularly of rice. The introduction of iron in around 800BC contributed significantly to these developments.

The kingdoms that ruled north India

2

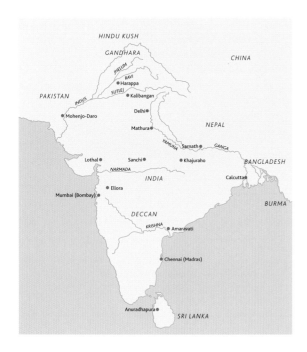

3

1 Stamp seal. From the Indus Valley. Steatite, c. 2000BC.
 Seals of this kind, carved with carefully rendered animals and inscriptions in an undeciphered script, survive in considerable quantities. They were apparently used for commercial purposes.

2 Miniature stupa-shaped reliquary. Sonala Pind Stupa, Manikiala, Punjab, Pakistan. Steatite, probably second century AD.
 This object once contained the relics of a Buddhist notable, along with coins of the period.

Indus civilisation 2500–1500BC			Life of the Buddha 563–483BC			
						Maurya 400–200BC
1750BC	1500BC	1250BC	1000BC	750BC	500BC	250BC

4

5

6

Kushan Empire (N) Satavahana (S) AD0–300	Gupta AD320–500 Huna invasion AD490–530	Medieval Indian Dynasties Pratihara AD600–950 Pala AD750–1150 Chola AD900–1200 Rashtrakuta AD600–1000	Islamic incursions (Afghanistan & Central Asia)	Delhi Sultanate AD1199–1526	Mughals from Central Asia Babur Hamayun Akbar Jahangir Awrangzeb	Late Mughal Period AD1707 –1857	Direct British Rule AD1857–1947
AD250	AD500	AD750	AD1000	AD1250	AD1500	AD1750	

7

at the time of the Buddha amalgamated into a single empire in the fourth century BC under Chandragupta, the first King of the Mauryan dynasty. The Mauryans introduced a formal system of writing and used stone for sculpture and architecture. Under Ashoka a series of royal edicts was engraved on pillars throughout this huge empire.

The Mauryan empire disintegrated after Ashoka's death, but Buddhism continued to flourish in the kingdoms emerging in the last two centuries BC. One of the most important ancient Buddhist sites of the time was Amaravati, in the Andhra country. The heavily embellished stupa there was surrounded by an elaborately carved stone railing.

The expansion of the Chinese Han empire into Central Asia drove nomadic tribes to migrate westward from the first to the fourth centuries AD. The most powerful of these were the Kushans, who established a vast empire from Central Asia and Afghanistan to Bihar and Bengal.

With the decline and disappearance of the Kushans in the early fourth century, many mutually hostile local rulers emerged. The final victor was Samudragupta, founder of the Gupta dynasty. Gupta rule marked a significant increase in cultural patronage: great temples were built and adorned with beautiful religious images. Leading centres of this art were at Sarnath and Mathura, the former a long-established Buddhist

8

centre, the latter a cosmopolitan city where all faiths prospered. The imperial formation of the Guptas was destroyed in the early sixth century by the White Huns from Central Asia.

The most important royal houses of medieval India were the Chalukyas, Rashtrakutas, Palas, Pallavas and Cholas. Their temples were richly endowed with lands, revenues and important fixed assets including ritual objects and precious metal images.

The end of temple wealth and prominence was heralded by the incursions of Mahmud of Ghazni in the late tenth century AD. In the late twelfth century, an ethnically Turkish, Islamic Sultanate was established in Delhi. The indigenous ruling elite that once built and endowed temples was increasingly circumscribed; temple lands were appropriated and many buildings fell into ruins. In courtly circles, Islamic practices from western Asia became the norm. Away from these centres, India remained tied to its traditional past with indigenous popular traditions based on ancient beliefs and practices, continuing little changed into the present era.

Another outside influence was the presence of European traders and colonists, who also began to arrive in the sixteenth century. Although by the mid-nineteenth century India had been absorbed into the British Empire, much of the subcontinent remained deeply traditional, and even now there is a thriving popular art tradition based on ancient beliefs and practices.

9

10

11

7 Shiva Nataraja. South India. Bronze, AD1100.
   Shiva is the lord of the cosmic dance in which he creates and destroys the universe, trampling Apasmara, the dwarf of ignorance, beneath his feet.

8 Tara. From Sri Lanka. Gilded bronze, eighth century AD.
   Tara is the greatest of all Buddhist goddesses and has a wide cult following. Here she makes the gesture of gift-giving or charity with her right hand.

9 Bodhisattva Avalokiteshvara. East India, ninth–tenth century AD.
   This deity has a seated Buddha in his hair and a lotus in his hand, and is widely worshipped as the supreme bodhisattva of compassion.

10 Bronze figure of Padmasambhava. Tibet, nineteenth century.
   Padmasambhava was an Indian monk who brought esoteric Buddhist teaching to Tibet in the eighth century AD.

11 A bronze figure of the Buddha, from Burma. Pagan period, c. AD1100.
   This form of the Buddha represents him at the moment of enlightenment, with his right hand reaching down to the earth which bears witness to the event.

Japan

Japanese culture has often been influenced by that of mainland Asia, but this should not obscure the antiquity of its indigenous civilisation. Indeed, the oldest datable pottery in the world is Japanese Jōmon ware from around 12,500BC. Jōmon means 'cord-marked' and refers to the patterns created by pressing cords into wet clay. Organised agriculture arrived in the third century BC, and the ensuing Yayoi period (300BC–AD300) saw the rapid adoption of technology from the mainland, including the use of the potter's wheel, weaving and bronze and iron casting. Bronze was normally used for ritual objects such as mirrors, spears and bells, while the harder iron was used for tools and, later, for weapons. Society became more settled and class-based, bound together by observance of the nascent Shintō religion. During the Kofun period (third–sixth century AD), the power of local ruling families spread to bring political unity to the greater part of the

islands. Material excavated from the burial mounds (kofun) of rulers, including haniwa, or clay guardians, has greatly increased our understanding of Kofun-period life and society, and in some cases has clarified the eighth-century written records.

Shintō, 'the way of the gods', was one of the strongest influences on the development of Japanese culture: with its emphasis on love and respect for the natural world, ancestors and craftsmanship, and on the inseparability of the physical and the spiritual, it played a large role in the adaptation and reinterpretation of ideas and techniques received from the mainland. Common Japanese stylistic traits, such as fondness for and inventive use of asymmetry, were also applied with great success to imported art forms such as lacquer.

Buddhism first came to Japan in the sixth century, though it continued to evolve long afterwards under successive waves of influence from the mainland.

1

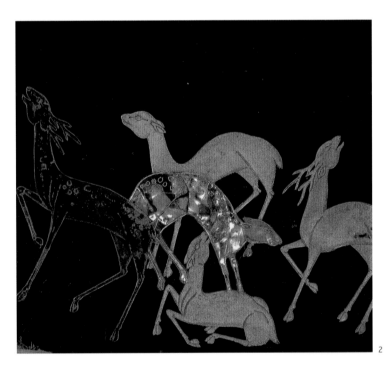

2

Jōmon period c.12,500BC – 300BC		Kofun period third–sixth century AD —
		Yayoi period 300BC–AD300

| 1000BC | 800BC | 600BC | 400BC | 200BC | 0 | AD200 |

Thus the intricate and formal court life of the Heian period (AD794–1185) was strongly coloured by the Tantric Shingon school, while the samurai warrior class which controlled the country from 1185 to 1868 favoured the disciplined and introspective Zen tradition imported from China and Korea. With its emphasis on contemplation and intuitive thought and action, Zen translated religious philosophy into aesthetic activities such as calligraphy, ink painting, interior and garden design, martial arts and the tea ceremony with its distinctive pottery styles. Japanese taste came to favour irregular shapes and asymmetric designs, exemplified by the Raku tea bowls first made by the potter Chōjirō for the great tea-master Sen no Rikyū in the late sixteenth century. The startling green, tan and white patterns of Oribe wares were also popular, as were the traditional natural ash glazes of the older kilns such as Bizen and Shigaraki.

With Buddhism came also the art of figural sculpture in wood. This reached its height during the Kamakura period (AD1185–1333) with the work of the Kei school. Earlier works had been carved from solid blocks of wood (*ichiboku-zukuri*), but Unkei, the thirteenth-century master, developed the *yosegi-zukuri*

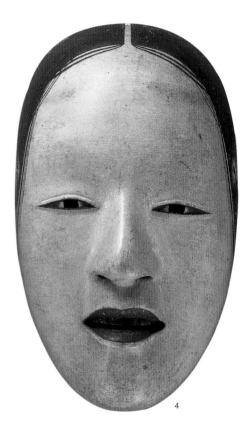

4

1 *Haniwa.* Low-fired red pottery, sixth century AD.

The nobility of the Kofun period were buried in impressive stone chambered tombs covered by huge mounds of earth. Pottery figures (*haniwa*) in the form of people, animals, birds and houses were placed around the outer slopes of the mound.

2 Lacquer writing box, seventeenth century AD.

By the 12th century, Japanese lacquerers had surpassed their Chinese and Korean predecessors, and lacquer was being widely used for domestic articles, furniture, ornaments and temple furnishings. From the sixteenth century onwards, lacquerware was produced for export and was avidly sought by Western collectors.

3 Wooden figure of Kichijōten, Female Deity of Fortune, Heian period, tenth century AD.

Kichijōten derived from the Hindu goddess Laksmi, the wife of Vishnu. She is associated with harvest, fertility and fortune. In Japan she later became one of the Seven Deities of Good Fortune. She is dressed as a lady of the Chinese Tang dynasty (618–906). The statue is carved from a single block of wood in *ichiboku-zukuri* style.

4 Noh mask. Painted wood, seventeenth–eighteenth century AD.

The 500-year-old Noh masked theatre tradition continues to flourish, and the British Museum collections include masks donated by living mask carvers. This example represents the character of a young woman.

Asuka period late-sixth century– AD710	Nara period AD710– 794	Heian period AD794–1185		Muromachi period AD1333–1573	Momoyama period AD1573– 1615		Modern period AD1868–
			Kamakura period AD1185–1333			Edo period AD1615–1868	
AD600	AD800	AD1000	AD1200	AD1400	AD1600	AD1800	

method of fixing together a number of hollowed segments, often producing larger, more animated figures. Skilled wood-carvers also developed the craft of carving masks for use in religious ritual and the ritual-based Noh theatre.

Metalworking techniques reached perfection in the work of swordsmiths. The production method of repeated folding, hammering and final heating and plunging in water produced tough weapons but also objects of great spiritual strength and beauty, the blade enhanced by a pattern of complex crystalline forms known as the *hamon*.

For over 200 years, from around 1639, Japan was relatively isolated from external influences. This encouraged the creation or elaboration of indigenous styles, particularly in ceramics and pictorial art. Porcelain production techniques had been introduced from the continent in the early seventeenth century. The industry, centred in Arita in southern Kyūshū, used porcelain clay that

had been discovered nearby. Native Japanese wares developed along very different lines from Chinese porcelains in terms of both style and function. From the 1660s onwards, Japanese porcelains were exported to Europe by the Dutch East India Company.

Painting schools that had grown up during the medieval period – such as the Tosa school, official painters to the imperial family and shoguns, and the Kano school, who served the temples and military aristocracy – continued to flourish in the Edo period (AD1615–1868), with the Kano artists dominating the painting world. Several new schools emerged, notably the Rimpa school with its ` highly decorative revival of courtly and literary themes, the Maruyama-Shijō school centred in Kyoto, and the literati, or *bunjin*, painters, who imitated 'amateur' works of the Chinese scholar-painters. Genre painting of everyday life and festivities developed into the Ukiyo-e school ('pictures of the floating world'), reflecting

5

6

the leisure pursuits, centred on urban pleasure quarters, of a rising wealthy merchant class. Prints and printed books of increasing complexity and sophistication were produced by Ukiyo-e artists. These also recorded the development of the popular Kabuki theatre.

The period of isolation was followed, from 1860 onwards, by a time of rapid and almost overwhelming Westernisation. However, the twentieth century saw a revival of confidence in such traditional art forms as ceramics and calligraphy. Today, there is also a flourishing school of Japanese-style painting (Nihonga), and Japanese prints, often very international in flavour, have a wide audience. Japan's rich regional traditions, including those of Okinawa and the Ainu in Hokkaidō, are now increasingly recognised.

7

8

5 'Tiger' hanging scroll by Maruyama Ōkyo, AD1775.

The hanging-scroll format originated in the Heian period as a means of displaying Buddhist paintings, and was later adopted by Zen ink painters. By Ōkyo's time, it had also become popular for purely secular subjects like this tiger.

6 Porcelain bowl, enamelled and decorated with patterns of azaleas, 1996.

This large, impressive bowl was made and donated by the Living National Treasure Sakaida Kakiemon, fourteenth in line from the Arita-based originator of Kakiemon-style porcelain, Sakaida Kizaemon (AD1596–1666). He created a distinctive orange-red, the colour of persimmons (kaki), which gives this style its name. There was a high demand for Kakiemon-type ware in seventeenth- and eighteenth-century Europe.

7 Katsushika Hokusai, 'South Wind, Clear Sky' ['Red Fuji'], colour woodblock print, AD 1830–33 From the series Thirty-Six Views of Mt Fuji.

It is said that when conditions are right in late summer or early autumn, with a wind from the south and a clear sky, the slopes of Fuji can appear dyed red by the rays of the rising sun. This is the most abstracted composition and yet the most meteorologically specific of Hokusai's series.

8 Tachi blade, fourteenth– fifteenth century AD, signed by Morokage of Bizen Province (present-day Okayama Prefecture).

Not only very efficient cutting weapons, Japanese swords were revered for their intrinsic beauty and spiritual qualities. They were also made and offered to shrines as gifts or vessels for the kami (gods), as well as being instruments of moral guidance to samurai warriors seeking the path to enlightenment. The hamon pattern of crystals on the blade is of the 'clove and reciprocating wave' type.

Korea

The Korean peninsula was already occupied in the Palaeolithic period; by Neolithic times, its inhabitants were producing comb-patterned pottery. Its Bronze Age was characterised by the construction of large cist graves and dolmens, as well as the introduction of rice cultivation. The bronzes produced at this time are quite different from those of China and include ritual implements used in shamanic ceremonies.

By 400BC, iron was being produced: considerable quantities of iron weapons and armour have been discovered in the south of the country. The high temperatures needed for iron production are associated with the emergence of stoneware pottery at this time. This period also saw the establishment of several Han Chinese colonies in the north. Korea was initially divided into four parts, but during the Three Kingdoms period (57BC–AD668), Kaya, in the central-southern part of the peninsula, was absorbed into Silla in the south-east. Koguryo occupied the north and Paekche the south-west.

In Koguryo, stone tombs built in the form of stepped pyramids contained chambers decorated with wall paintings strongly influenced by those of Han China. Paekche had maritime contacts with southern China and also influenced the development of Buddhist art in Japan, where many of its artists and craftsmen emigrated. The dramatic stoneware funerary vessels produced in Kaya and Silla were probably used in shamanistic burial rituals. Silla tombs have also yielded spectacular sheet-gold crowns, belts, shoes, earrings and vessels whose decoration may indicate an origin in the Scytho-Siberian steppe cultures of Central Asia.

Silla unified Korea in AD668; its splendid capital at Kyongju was based on the Tang Chinese capital at Chang-an. Close relations with China led to the introduction of a Chinese-style administration, and many Koreans travelled to China and beyond. The highly stratified society of the Unified Silla period persisted under the Koryŏ dynasty (AD918–1392), under whose rule the Buddhist church grew in both influence and wealth. Many fine works of art – paintings, illuminated manuscripts, sculptures and celadon wares – were produced for the glory of Buddhism.

Reproduction of the Buddhist scriptures was considered a meritorious act; in the eleventh century, the entire canon was printed from over 80,000 hand-carved woodblocks, an extraordinary accomplishment carried out in a vain attempt to protect Korea from invasion by the Mongols. The desire to print holy texts more quickly and efficiently led to the invention of movable metal type – the earliest in the world – in the early thirteenth century.

Buddhism was persecuted during the long Chosŏn dynasty (AD1392–1910), when strict Confucianism was the prevailing philosophy. The fifteenth century, however, saw a flowering of science, technology and culture, though a series of Japanese invasions at the end of the sixteenth century caused great destruction. No sooner had Korea recovered from these incursions – sometimes called the 'Pottery Wars' because the Japanese took many potters as prisoners – than it was invaded by the Manchus, who were to form the Chinese Qing dynasty. However, the fact that the eighteenth century was a period of confident maturity is reflected in the art of the time.

1

Neolithic 6000–1000BC								Iron Age – Proto Three Kingdoms 400BC–AD300
				Bronze Age 1000–200BC				

| 3000BC | 2500BC | 2000BC | 1500BC | 1000BC | 800BC | 600BC | 400BC | 200BC | 0 |

2

3

4

5

1 Water sprinkler (*kundika*). Porcelain with white-slip inlay and celadon glaze. Koryŏ dynasty, twelfth century AD.

Water sprinklers like this were used in Buddhist rituals. The vessel shape originated in India, and the technique of making translucent celadon glazes was imported from China, but the inlay technique was a Korean innovation.

2 Portrait of a Confucian scholar. Ink and colours on paper. Chosŏn dynasty, late eighteenth–nineteenth century AD.

The scholar is shown dressed in traditional white clothes and a hat made of woven horsehair. The detailed portrayal of the face shows Western influence introduced via Jesuit painters at the Chinese court in Beijing, which was visited by Korean painters and envoys.

3 Illuminated manuscript of the *Amitābhā sūtra*. Gold and silver paint on blue paper, Koryŏ dynasty, dated AD1341.

The discourses of the Buddha are known as *sutra*, the commentaries on them *abidharma* and the rules of monastic conduct as *vinaya*. These comprise the three main branches of the Buddhist canon. The only illustration in this copy of the *Amitābhā sūtra*, this painting shows the Buddha preaching.

4 Bronze belt buckle in the shape of a horse. Early Iron Age, second–first century BC.

Animal-shaped belt buckles are thought to have been status symbols.

5 Gold earrings. Three Kingdoms Period, fifth–seventh century AD.

Probably from a Silla royal tomb, these are unusual pieces in Western collections.

	Unified Silla AD668–935		Japanese occupation AD1910–1945
Three Kingdoms 57BC–AD668		Koryŏ AD918–1392	
Koguryo 37BC–AD668			
Paekche 18BC–AD663			
Kaya AD42–562		Chosŏn (Yi) AD1392–1910	
Silla 57BC–AD668			

| 200 | AD400 | AD600 | AD800 | AD1000 | AD1200 | AD1400 | AD1600 | AD1800 | AD2000 |

The Pacific & Australia

The great expanse of the Pacific Ocean is inhabited space. At the beginning of the 21st century, more than 14,000,000 people live in 28 nations spread across the Pacific, between them speaking more than 1,300 languages. For many of these people, the ocean is not so much a barrier as a known landscape across which they travel constantly by boat or plane, exchanging goods and knowledge and extending and maintaining personal and family networks. Pacific islanders have always been skilled navigators and linguists. As the scholar Epeli Hau'ofa describes his Pacific ancestors: '. . . their universe comprised not only land surfaces, but the surrounding ocean as far as they could traverse and exploit it, the underworld with its fire-controlling and earth-shaking denizens, and the heavens above with their hierarchies of powerful gods and named stars and constellations that people could count on to guide their ways across the seas' (1994).

The Spanish and Portuguese began exploring the scattered islands of the northern Pacific through the sixteenth and seventeenth centuries. The *Antelope*, a British East India Company ship, ran aground near the island of Palau in 1783: items the Palauans gave the sailors

are now in the Museum, which is unusual in holding a significant collection from the northern Pacific. The first European encounters with the wider Pacific focused on the islands in the east, such as Tahiti, New Zealand and Hawaii. Europeans found these societies easy to deal with: their complex social structures with leaders, commoners and priests were not dissimilar, for example, to the eighteenth-century English class system. Moreover, eastern Pacific islanders were keen to engage in exchanges of all kinds. The Museum's collections include material acquired by early visitors to the eastern Pacific such as Captain James Cook, who was given an elaborate Tahitian mourner's costume on his second voyage (AD 1772–5). Missionaries followed the first explorers, the London Missionary Society arriving in 1797, and made collections. The figure known as A'a, representing a deity in the Austral Islands (south-eastern Pacific), was presented to LMS missionaries in 1821. Today, most Pacific nations are firmly Christian.

Cultures everywhere are always evolving in response to people's preferences and circumstances, but Europeans brought disease and other destructive forces to the Pacific, and many populations

1

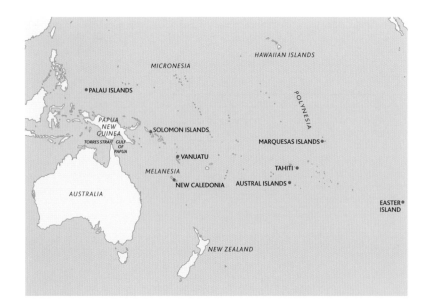

1 | Wood figure representing the Polynesian deity A'a, the progenitor of the island of Rurutu, Austral Islands. A large cavity in the figure's back once contained 24 smaller images, now lost. Acquired in 1911, it is one of the finest and most famous examples of Polynesian sculpture in existence.

3

2 Large stone figure (Hoa Hakananai'a). Orongo, Easter Island. Such figures, commemorating important ancestors, were produced between 1000BC and the second half of the seventeenth century.

3 Carved board. Elema people, eastern Gulf Province, Papua New Guinea.

This board was made to house a forest spirit and was kept in the communal men's house. The Elema set out to entertain and amuse forest spirits as well as to benefit from their assistance. The figure depicted is probably dancing. He wears regalia including a pearl-shell chest ornament and bark belt.

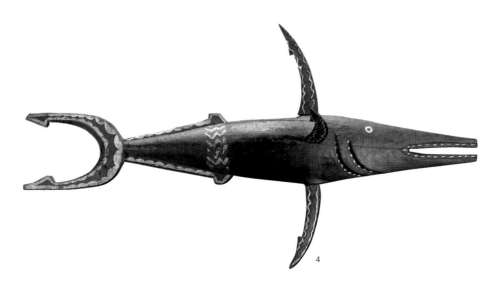

4

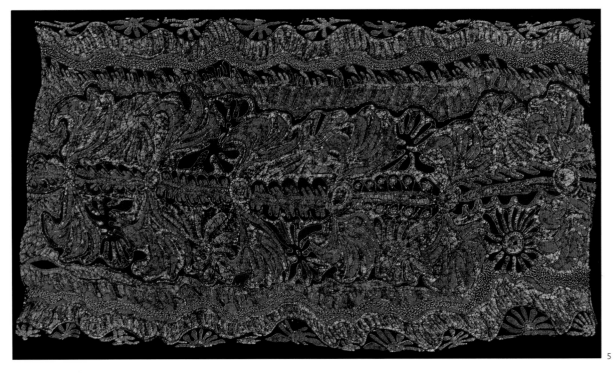

5

and practices declined or disappeared under these pressures. The famous stone figure from Rapanui (Easter Island) known as Hoa Hakananai'a was probably originally located outside with other similar figures. Several hundred years later, it was moved into a stone house at a ritual centre, and bas-relief designs were carved and painted on its back, suggesting a new and special role. It was collected in 1868, when the Rapanui population was much reduced. The late twentieth century saw a reassertion of Pacific identity and culture, and objects made and collected in the past are often very significant to populations today. Hoa Hakananai'a is a good example of this.

In the western Pacific islands, immediately north and east of Australia, people characteristically organised themselves into small societies. These groups were linked by sophisticated networks of trade and exchange, which continue, in modified form, within the nations of Papua New Guinea, the Solomon Islands and Vanuatu and in New Caledonia. The much more egalitarian social systems of the western Pacific were difficult for Europeans to understand. Partly because there were no powerful leaders interested in guaranteeing the Europeans' safety, people here seemed less welcoming than in the islands to the east. The earliest British Museum collections from this region date from the 1830s; more material was acquired through colonial officials and missionaries in the late nineteenth century. The wooden fish-shaped container for a human skull from Santa Ana in the Solomon Islands was collected by Admiral Davis on one of the British naval patrols attempting to regulate European dealings with islanders (AD 1890–93). The carved and painted board from the Elema people of the Gulf of Papua was, by contrast, collected by James Chalmers of the LMS in 1914.

Indigenous Australians have been living on that continent for more than 40,000 years. There were at least 250 language groups at the time of the first European settlement, many of which have not survived. Whereas Pacific islanders were and are agriculturalists, growing crops in food gardens, Aboriginal Australians had a sophisticated knowledge of their environments which allowed them to hunt and harvest what they needed. Their complex religious and philosophical understandings are today partly channelled into art. This includes paintings on bark, canvas and fabric, using traditional and imported techniques, and depicts stories, beliefs and landscape. Through art, Aboriginal Australians assert their continuing presence in Australia, as well as their cultural vibrancy.

6

7

4 Skull container. Santa Ana, Makira Province, Solomon Islands.

This carved fish (a shark or a bonito) contained the skull of an important ancestor. Potent relics such as this allowed communities to draw on the assistance of the dead. Ghosts were sometimes incarnated in living sharks. This container was sold to the Museum in 1904.

5 Contemporary batik on silk by Nyukana Baker. From Ernabella in central Australia.

In Australia indigenous designs and ways of depicting the world are now being explored using new media such as batik on silk. Baker is an artist who has exhibited widely both within and outside her country.

6 Nephrite neck pendant, *hei tiki*. Maori, New Zealand.

Nephrite has always been prized by the Maori and was used for prestigious weapons and personal ornaments. Such objects are treasured heirlooms and are handed down from generation to generation, acquiring more spiritual power with each successive owner.

7 *Parae*, chief mourner's dress. Tahiti.

After the death of a person of high rank, a near relative or priest would traverse the surrounding district wearing such a masked costume and brandishing a tooth-edged club. The passage of the chief mourner may have marked the passage of the deceased's spirit to the world of the dead. As the mourner approached, people hid to avoid his power and violence. This costume, which includes pearl-shell, feathers, bark-cloth, wood and coconut shell, was probably given to Captain James Cook in 1774.

Mesoamerica, Central & South America

The term *Mesoamerica* was coined by the anthropologist Paul Kirchhoff in the 1940s to describe a large area of southern North America and Central America that once shared similar cultural traits. This area encompasses modern Mexico, Guatemala, Belize, El Salvador and western Honduras and Nicaragua, although its frontiers have fluctuated through time. From the desert of northern Mexico to the tropical Pacific coast in the south-east, this ecologically diverse region saw the rise of numerous cultural traditions with a common world view.

The earliest evidence for agriculture in Mesoamerica comes from the state of Guerrero in Mexico. Maize, the staple crop, had been fully domesticated by the fourth millennium BC. Agricultural communities grew in numbers and complexity throughout Mesoamerica during the Preclassic (c. 2500 BC–AD 250), a period that also saw the emergence of pottery.

One of the earliest known civilisations was that of the Olmec (1200–400 BC). The southern Gulf Coast was the heartland of

Olmec culture, which produced large architectural complexes, monumental sculpture and fine lapidary work. It is also in this area that we find the earliest evidence of the Mesoamerican calendar, in the second century BC, and a pantheon of deities that formed the basis of what later developed into a pan-Mesoamerican religion that would last until the Spanish conquest in the sixteenth century.

The city of Teotihuacan, in the Basin of Mexico, emerged as a centre of religious, commercial and civic power during the Classic period (c. AD250–900). This large metropolis exerted a widespread influence. At the time, in the Maya area, population increase marked the growth of urban centres, especially in the Lowlands. The large number of Classic Maya hieroglyphic inscriptions, carved on stone monuments, suggests a complex mosaic of political alliances and warfare among numerous city-states.

During the Postclassic (c. AD900–1521), changes in political and economic alignments become evident. There was an increase in militarism and a shift in long-

1

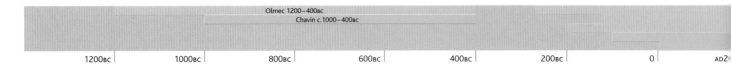

Olmec 1200–400BC

Chavin c.1000–400BC

| 1200BC | 1000BC | 800BC | 600BC | 400BC | 200BC | 0 | AD2 |

1 Votive jade axe. Olmec, 1200–400BC.

This massive ceremonial axe combines character-istics of the caiman and the jaguar, the most powerful predators of the tropical lowlands. The V-shaped cleft in the head signals its power to penetrate the underworld.

2 Hollow pottery figure. West Mexico c. 300BC–AD300.

Modelled figures are found as offerings in deep shaft tombs reserved for the élite. They portray fauna, flora, and lively scenes from everyday life including people eating, drinking or playing musical instruments.

3 Carved stone lintel. From Yaxchilan, Mexico. Maya, Late Classic period, (AD600–900).

Lintel 15 is one of a series of three that commemorates the accession to power of Bird Jaguar IV, a powerful Maya ruler. It illustrates a blood-letting rite performed by one of his wives.

4 Turquoise mosaic repre-senting a double-headed serpent. Aztec/Mixtec c. AD1500.

Mixtec artisans excelled in lapidary/stone work. Shell, turquoise and other precious stones were used to fashion masks, shields, staffs and ornaments, usually reserved for the use of the elite or to represent deities.

	Maya 250BC–AD1000		
Teotihuacan 150BC–AD750		Huastec AD900–1450	
Zapotec 200BC–AD800			Mixtec AD1200–1521
oché 100BC–AD700			Aztec AD1300–1521
Nasca AD1–700	Quimbaya AD400–900	Chimú AD900–1470	Inca AD1438–1532

| AD400 | AD600 | AD800 | AD1000 | AD1200 | AD1400 | AD1600 |

5

6

distance trade routes. It was during this period that the Aztecs dominated the central highlands, ranging, from the Gulf Coast to the Pacific, and exacted tribute from conquered provinces. The Aztecs (also known as the Mexica) had risen – through a combination of dynastic alliance, trade and conquest – from humble beginnings in AD1325 to become a large empire by the time the Spaniards arrived in the sixteenth century.

Contacts between Mesoamerica and Central and South America are evident at different periods. Pottery and funerary architecture in West Mexico indicate contacts with Ecuador and Colombia at the end of the Preclassic, while the technology of metalworking was introduced from northern South America via the isthmus of Central America (Panama and Costa Rica) in the Postclassic period. One route of entry was by way of the Maya

area into Central Mexico and adjacent regions. A second point of introduction was the coast of West Mexico and into the adjacent hinterland. The peoples of Colombia and Peru also produced fine metalwork in gold, silver, copper and bronze, including the exceptionally beautiful cast ornaments in the Quimbaya style of Colombia.

The Andes and the fertile valleys which cut across the arid desert coast of Peru provided a dramatic backdrop for a succession of cultures. Pottery appeared on the coast of Ecuador in the fourth millennium BC and in northern and central Peru in the second millennium BC. However, the presence of luxury items, especially textiles, and monumental architecture actually predated the use of ceramics. In northern Peru, monumental structures were erected at Chavin de Huantar over 2,500 years ago; Chavin

culture exerted far-reaching political and religious control.

During the so-called Early Intermediate period (200BC–AD 600), the Moché rose to prominence in the north, erecting large architectural complexes in their capital at Cerro Blanco. One of these, Huaca del Sol, is the largest adobe structure ever built in the Andes. The ceramics the Moché produced include stirrup-spout vessels decorated with fine-line painting and polychrome vessels representing realistic portrait heads.

On the south coast, the Nasca are best known for their beautiful polychrome pottery and textiles decorated with a great variety of animals and geometric patterns. The Nasca Lines (large figures drawn in the desert) represent some of the same motifs.

In the *altiplano* close to Lake Titicaca, Tiwanaku exercised control until the end of the first millennium AD. Monumental structures, gateways and stelae testify to the influence of this great religious centre.

The most powerful empire in South America was that of the Inca (c. 1200–1535), which extended from modern Ecuador to Chile. Their architecture is truly remarkable: large blocks of stone tightly fitted together to form houses, palaces and religious structures. The Spanish destruction of the Inca empire and its capital, Cusco, in 1534 signalled an abrupt end to an accomplished civilisation that had boasted its own calendar, an extraordinary network of roads and a sophisticated and highly productive agricultural system of terraces and irrigation canals.

7

8

9

5	Pottery whistling vessel. Peru, Chimú AD900–1470.

The Chimú produced a distinctive black pottery, using a particular firing technique and then burnishing the vessels. A couple engaged in an energetic dance is modelled on top of one of the chambers.

6	Pottery vessel. Moché, AD100–700.

The ceramics of the Moché culture of coastal Peru were exceptionally sophisticated in both technique and design. This portrait vessel accurately captures the forbidding countenance of a powerful lord.

7	Nasca vessel with hummingbirds, 200BC–AD600.

This motif, representing hummingbirds hovering around flowers at the base of the spouts, is characteristic of the early phases of the Nasca cultural sequence. Hummingbirds are considered to be the intermediaries or even manifestations of mountain gods.

8	Gold llama. Peru. Inca, c. AD1400–1532.

Small figurines representing humans and llamas, have been found at Inca mountain-top shrines, temples and human burials, deposited as offerings. This llama is made of a thin sheet of gold, hammered into shape and soldered at the joints.

9	Lime flask made of tumbaga (a gold-copper alloy). Quimbaya style, AD400–900.

The figure is hollow, with an opening on top of the head, and served as a ritual container for lime powder. The lime was chewed with coca leaves to release their active stimulant.

North America

There are two interpretations for the original peopling of the Americas. Archaeologists and linguists describe a population flow into the area between 15,000 and 40,000 years ago during the last Ice Age, when sea levels were much lower. What is now the Bering Strait formed a vast land-bridge linking Alaska with Siberia; hunters in pursuit of big game such as mammoths crossed from Asia into Alaska, spreading quickly through both American continents, either along the coast or through the interior. The thousand or so Native peoples have a quite different interpretation of their origins, conveyed through varied oral histories and often related to their ancestral territories or current tribal lands. Linguistic diversity – perhaps 25 per cent of the world's languages are North American – characterised the continent before European contact.

The rapid spread of population was accompanied by the development of specialised tool kits and lifestyles suited to the varied niche environments of North America. Horticulture, for instance, developed more than 2,000 years ago, prompted by the intensive gathering of wild grains, gourds and seeds. Farming and the establishment of long-distance trade

routes encouraged the growth of distinct, complex cultures, such as those of the Adena and Hopewell peoples of the Ohio Valley during the Woodland period. The Adena constructed conical burial mounds, while the Hopewell are renowned for their vast earthworks, defensive and ceremonial in use, especially in the Ohio Valley.

Mesoamerican influence a thousand years ago became particularly important in the southern US with the arrival of staple crops such as maize from Mexico. This is known as the Mississippian period and is characterised by a flourishing agricultural civilisation featuring the construction of ceremonial sites with vast flat-topped pyramids, or temple mounds, and courts for ball games. One of the main cities, Cahokia, Illinois, had a population of between 10,000 and 20,000 people in the eleventh century, similar to that of London at the time. In the Southwest, highly specialised farming cultures, with varied irrigation systems, developed to cope with desert conditions. Puebloan peoples, like the Hopi today, maintained their language and culture without being overwhelmed by Euro-American society. For the people of this region, the seasonal arrival of

1

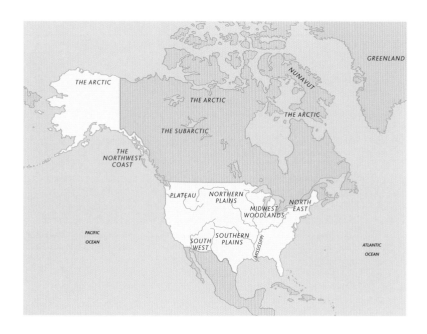

2

rain was and remains a matter of over-whelming importance, invoked to this day in song and ceremony, and depicted in art.

Throughout the continent, however, hunting remained an important source of food. During the last millennium or two, the Inupiat and Inuit of the Arctic coasts have specialised in the pursuit of marine mammals such as seal, walrus and whale. In a land frozen for most of the year, mobility by sled and in kayaks was vital to maintain food supplies. Today, snow-mobiles provide the transport of choice in settled communities, which often consist of self-governing territories as in Greenland and Nunavut. The introduction of the horse by the Spanish colonists in New Mexico after 1598 eventually enabled the peoples of the Plains to hunt bison more effectively, providing Indians with food as well as skins for clothing and tipis. After the disappearance of the bison in the 1880s, Indians turned from hunting to ranching. This had mixed success owing

3

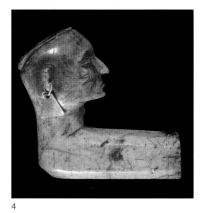
4

5

1 Crow wool dress. Montana, *c.* 1900.	**2** Ivory arrowshaft straightener, carved with two foetal caribou heads and engraved with scenes of dancing and hunting. Inupiat, Alaska, *c.* 1850.	**3** Headdress of Yellow Calf. Immature golden eagle feathers, red trade cloth, glass beads, skin and horse hair. Arapaho, Wyoming, *c.* 1900.	**4** Soapstone pipe bowl used by the American painter Benjamin West in his historical paintings of America, southern Great Lakes, *c.* 1765.	**5** Hopewell smoking pipe from Mound City, Ohio, depicting a bird of prey eating a fish. Stone, *c.* AD 100–600.
The elk teeth decorating this garment are indicative of the hunting prowess of the wearer's husband.	The caribou images have amuletic significance.			Such zoomorphic images may represent the protective spirits of clans or high-ranking individuals.

in part to the enforced transfer of Native land, by the allotment process, to non-Natives. At the same time, numerous other cultural restrictions were enforced, including the prohibition of the use of Native languages in Indian schools and restrictions on ceremonial and religious events such as the Sun Dance.

In the North and Northeast, the supply of furs to European traders became a staple economic activity, replacing or complementing the traditional hunt. On the Northwest Coast, abundant resources, particularly of different species of salmon and other marine animals, ensured (and continue to provide) ample food for the maintenance of sedentary fishing peoples. These hierarchical societies continue to maintain status through the celebration of clan, family and lineage stories of origin. At elaborate feasts called potlatches, traditionally celebrated in winter, life-cycle events are commemorated with powerful songs and danced re-enactments of family origin myths in the animal world. These usually include masked performances.

The first Europeans arrived in Greenland and Newfoundland in the tenth century AD, but settlement did not begin in earnest until the seventeenth century. Drawn by the twin goals of obtaining land and furs, settlers penetrated the continent along the great rivers of the eastern seaboard. The Native population was devastated by introduced diseases and, through the eighteenth century, by catastrophic colonial wars between the Americans, British and French. During the nineteenth century, European Americans and Canadians displaced the indigenous population, forcing Indians onto reservations and reserves. Today, economic and cultural revival, best exemplfied by dynamic artistic traditions and by pow-wow celebrations, is accompanied by rapidly growing populations, developing economic self-sufficiency and the assumption of a degree of self-government by many Native Nations.

6

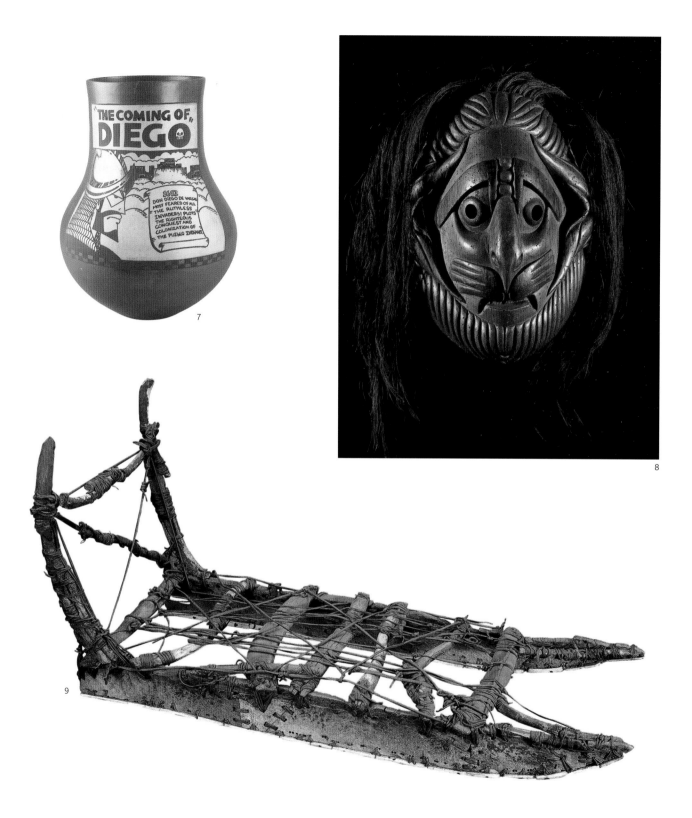

7

8

9

6 Chilkat Tlingit blanket or cloak. Twined of mountain-goat wool and cedar bark, with a crest, possibly a diving whale. Alaska, nineteenth century.

7 'The Coming of Diego', a pot by Cochiti artist Diego Romero, New Mexico, 1995, commemorating the Pueblo Revolt (1680–92) and showing the reconquest by Don Diego de Vargas (in comic book style).

8 Nulthamalth, or fool dancer, mask worn to help enforce correct behaviour at potlatches or feasts. Kwakwaka'wakw, British Columbia, c. 1850.

9 Polar Inuit sled carved in a timberless land from bone and ivory, and tied together with skin thongs. North Greenland, c. 1818.

Prehistoric Europe

Humans came to Europe almost a million years ago, bringing with them the stone-working skills and hunter-gatherer lifestyle of their African ancestors. Fully modern people, *Homo sapiens sapiens*, did not arrive until about 40,000 years ago, during the last Ice Age. The ensuing period – the Upper Palaeolithic – saw not only technological advances in stone tools and weaponry but the appearance of personal ornaments and art: animals, humans and symbols were painted, sculpted or engraved on cave walls, pieces of bone, antler, ivory and stone.

Towards the end of the Ice Age, an entirely different relationship with the natural world evolved. Agriculture developed in the Middle East about 11,000 years ago and spread across Europe, reaching its western regions by 4000BC. Life became more settled and work more specialised. New tools for working the land were created in stone and wood, and pottery vessels were made to store the food grown.

As more complex societies emerged, eastern European art turned towards the representation of the human form, though the highly stylised surviving examples suggest superhuman or ideal models rather than ordinary humans. In western regions, large stone structures ranging from single standing stones to the imposing complex at Stonehenge began to be erected. The earliest trackways, built to assist the seasonal movements of herders, also date from this period.

Expanding populations and steadily improving communications brought more trade and contact, but also more friction between social groups. Originating in Anatolia, copper metallurgy was stimulated in areas of southern Europe from the later fifth millennium BC onwards. Only much later, around 2500BC, did this new technology make an impact on the further corners of Europe and the British Isles, adding new dimensions to social ranking, the expression of identities and the control of resources. Bronze, the product of alloying tin with copper, began to come into use from around 2300BC, but was not the universal alloy for some centuries because of scarce tin sources in Europe.

While literate and civilised societies grew up around the eastern Mediterranean, in the greater part of Europe tribal

1

2

Neolithic 6000–2000 BC				Later Bronze Age 1500–700 BC
		Earlier Bronze Age 2000–1500 BC		
2250BC	2000BC	1750BC	1500BC	

		Hallstatt B 800–700 BC			Iron Age – Hallstatt C–D and La Tène 700 BC–AD43		
	Hallstatt A 1100–800 BC						
		Villanovans		Etruscans			
1000 BC		750 BC		500 BC		250 BC	0

6

7

structures continued to evolve, under-pinned sometimes by religious authority, sometimes by élite trade networks and sometimes by martial supremacy. Material culture varied enormously over the continent, but on occasion, as with the trappings of the 'Beaker culture' across western Europe, particular forms spread through otherwise disparate societies. Considerable numbers of pots and fine artefacts of flint, bronze, gold and other exotic materials were buried in hoards, offered to water deities or placed with the dead as part of varied burial rites.

By the time iron replaced bronze to make tools and weapons 2,800 years ago, Europe was a patchwork of complex farming communities that lived without cities, money or states. There was con-siderable trade and contact between farming societies, especially for the necessities of life such as iron and salt. Many of these farmers were also warriors, and some places were ruled by chiefs or even kings. Warfare, chariots and feasting were often important aspects of life for

which skilled craftspeople made elaborate decorated objects such as weapons, horse harness and wine flagons. These objects are found today because many were placed in graves and others were offered to the gods.

From about 2,500 years ago, a new abstract style of art began which we call La Tène or Early Celtic art today. From this time onwards, peoples of northern Europe increasingly came into contact with the Greeks and Romans because of trade, war-fare and conquest. It is from the writings of Greeks and Romans that we begin to learn the names, languages and histories of peoples they called Celts, Germans, Iberians and Britons. As the Roman Empire grew, there were also changes in lifestyles and society among farming peoples in the rest of Europe. In some places, towns, coins and writing appeared, along with changes in farming, crafts and art.

In Italy, the Iron Age took a different turn, though areas of the north had strong affinities with 'Celtic' northern Europe. In the west of the peninsula and in the Po

9

Valley, the Proto-Etruscan culture showed early signs of urbanisation in the ninth century BC. Contact with Phoenician traders and the Greek colonists who settled in the south and west from the eighth century onwards introduced exotic imports from parts of the eastern Mediterranean, and as true cities grew up, powerful local aristocracies emerged. The Etruscans, who wrote in an alphabet derived from Greek and buried their dead in magnificent tombs, were never united politically, but extended their influence north over the Apennines and south into Campania. The southern and central regions were peopled by many other tribal groups, among them those later known as Sabines, Samnites, Daunians and Peucetians.

In Latium, to the south of the area inhabited by the Proto-Etruscans, a powerful city-dwelling people – the Latins – began to expand their power from the seventh and sixth centuries BC onwards. Their greatest city, Rome, bequeathed their language and traditions to the next great empire of ancient Europe.

10

| 6 | The Great Torc. From Snettisham, Norfolk, first century BC.
A characteristic 'Celtic' ornament, the torc is a heavy neck-ring made of twisted metal. This fine example is made of eight gold strands, each strand comprising eight wires. The ends are secured in elaborately decorated cast gold terminals. | 7 | Bronze flagon. From Basse-Yutz, France, c. 400 BC.
One of a pair decorated with inlays of coral and red enamel, this flagon is one of the outstanding examples of early 'Celtic' art of the La Tène period. | 8 | Etruscan bronze mirror-back, c. 350–300 BC.
The engraving of legendary scenes on the backs of mirrors was one of the most highly developed forms of Etruscan art. This example shows the hero Perseus regarding the severed head of the Gorgon Medusa. | 9 | Gold stater of Commius, c. 40–20 BC.
Greek coinage was copied by the Iron Age peoples of central and northern Europe from the third or second century BC; by the mid-first century, the practice had spread to Britain. Commius was a king of the southern British tribe of the Atrebates. | 10 | The Battersea Shield, first century BC. Found in the River Thames at Battersea, London.
This bronze facing from a wooden shield is decorated with flowing palmette and scroll designs enhanced with red enamel. The shield was probably deliberately consigned to the river as a ceremonial dedication. |

The Greek World

The ancient Greek world occupied a large area of the eastern Mediterranean from the Early Bronze Age to Roman times. In the later fourth millennium BC, the Cycladic Islands in the Aegean saw the birth of a distinctive culture producing simple marble figurines, fine stone vessels and painted pottery. During the later third and early second millennia BC, the focus of Aegean civilisation shifted south to the Minoan culture of Crete, named after the island's legendary King Minos. Minoan wealth and prestige are evident in the architectural splendour of the palace at Knossos and in the fine Minoan jewellery, engraved gems and seals found throughout the Aegean. In mainland Greece, a related civilisation at Mycenae and other sites of the Peloponnese survived into the late twelfth century BC.

The people of the Mycenaean culture were linguistically related to the Greeks of later eras, and the linear script in which they kept their official accounts has been interpreted as an early form of Greek. The epics of Homer and other tales that later Greeks told of this period were written down long after reliable memories of it had faded.

For the Greek world, the period that followed the early Iron Age was an unsettled time of depopulation and migration. Its pottery is characterised by striking geometric patterns, but by about 700BC,

1

2

	Early Cycladic I–III		Middle Cycladic I–III
	Early Minoan I–III		Middle Minoan I–III
	Early Helladic I–III		Middle Helladic
3000BC	2750BC	2500BC	2000BC

3

4

5

<table>
<tr><td>1</td><td>Marble Cycladic figurine, c. 2700–2500BC. Early Spedos type.

There are traces of paint indicating facial features, a diadem and a pattern of dots on one of the cheeks.</td><td>2</td><td>Mycenaean two-handled crater or jar, painted with a series of chariots, 1350–1325BC.

This jar was found on Cyprus, where such Mycenaean products were particularly popular.</td><td>3</td><td>The 'Master of the Animals', Minoan gold pendant from the Aegina Treasure, c. 1700–1500BC.

The figure holds a water-fowl in each hand and is flanked by stylised plant-like elements.</td><td>4</td><td>Silver tetradrachm coin of Athens, 450–406BC.

The history of coinage has its origins in the Greek world of the early seventh century BC: the first metal coin was struck in the kingdom of Lydia in western Turkey c. 625BC.</td><td>5</td><td>Part of a colossal limestone statue of a bearded priest. Archaic, 500–480BC, from the Sanctuary of Apollo at Idalion, Cyprus.

The figure would have been placed alongside a series of similar statues at the front of the main court of the sanctuary.</td></tr>
</table>

				Geometric period	Reforms of Kleisthenes, birth of democracy 508BC
	Late Minoan I–III			First recorded Olympic games at Olympia 776BC	Archaic period
	Late Helladic				
1500BC		1250BC		1000BC	750BC

6

7

figurative art was returning. Phoenician traders had already brought alphabetic writing to Greece; now, contact with the East reintroduced the Greeks to the art of human representation. Small bronze statuettes, larger marble figures possibly inspired by Egyptian models and vase painting – first in black on a red background, then (from the late sixth century onwards) red on black – illustrate the development of the exploration of the human form as the central and most enduring aspect of Greek art.

Archaic Greece was a world of city-states interconnected by political and historical bonds such as those linking the many colonies of Italy, Sicily and Asia Minor to their mainland mother cities. These states were sometimes ruled by individual 'tyrants' who established themselves and their families as heads of government. More often, affairs were controlled by a small group of well-born men, or oligarchs. Elsewhere, decisions were made by the whole citizenry: all free, native, adult males. This was democracy, seen in its purest form at Athens in the mid-fifth century BC.

Democratic Athens is often regarded as typifying Greece's Classical age. The city's role in saving the mainland from conquest by Persia in 480BC and its

6 Athenian black-figured amphora signed by Exekias as potter, c. 540–530BC, showing Achilles killing Penthesileia, queen of the Amazons. Found at Vulci, Italy.

According to Greek myth Achilles fell in love with Penthesileia at the moment she died.

7 Athenian red-figured vase, 480–470BC, showing the scene from Homer's *Odyssey* in which the hero Odysseus is bound to the mast of his ship so that he can listen to the Sirens' songs without being enticed away by them.

Persian invasions of Greek mainland 512–479BC	480BC Battle of Salamis, Persians defeated at sea 479BC Battle of Plataea, Persians defeated on land	404BC Athens defeated by Sparta	c. 350BC Mausoleum of Halikarnassos built
	480BC Athens sacked by Persians 447–432BC Parthenon constructed	Classical period	323BC Death of Alexander the Great
	450BC	400BC	350BC	300BC

8

9

The Parthenon Sculptures

Dedicated to Athena, the city's patron goddess, the Parthenon was the most important temple in ancient Athens. Built in the mid-fifth century BC, its architects were Iktinos and Kallikrates and the famous sculptor Pheidias oversaw the carved decoration. Brought to England by Lord Elgin in the early nineteenth century, the sculptures are sometimes known as the Elgin Marbles. They include a large number of blocks from the frieze that ran around the temple exterior, together with some fragmentary sculptures from the pediments and some of the metopes from the temple's south side. The frieze, portraying a long procession of horsemen and votaries, has been interpreted as representing the Great Panathenaia, a festival held every four years.

8 | Etruscan bronze helmet dedicated at Olympia.
The inscription records the defeat of the Etruscans by the Syracusans under their tyrant, Hieron, in a sea battle in 474BC.

9 | A woman-headed bird (or Siren) clutching a small human figure. From the 'Harpy Tomb' at Xanthos, Lykia, 470–460BC.
In Greek myth and art Sirens helped to escort the dead to the Underworld and guarded their tombs.

Hellenistic period

Battle of Actium 31BC
Death of Cleopatra VII, last of Hellenistic monarchs

200BC   150BC   100BC   50BC

10

acquisition of a wealthy Aegean empire, as recorded by the historian Thucydides, ensured Athens' political prominence until its defeat by Sparta in 404BC. Fifth-century Athens was a haven for philosophers, dramatists and artists such as Sokrates and Aristophanes. This coincidence of imperial wealth and artistic splendour found brilliant expression in the Parthenon and other buildings of the Acropolis.

Elsewhere in the Greek world, a variety of political systems coexisted. In Asia Minor, these ranged from the rule of local tyrants to the semi-independent rule established by the priests of powerful temples or sanctuaries. In Sicily, too, autocracy was the order of the day: in Syracuse, the triumph of tyranny over democracy brought the city great power and influence over the whole island and much of southern Italy. Such regimes were often just as favourable to advances in philosophy, art and science as democracy

had been: Syracuse provided a home for Plato, while his pupil Aristotle lived for some years in the little tyranny of Atarneus in Asia Minor. All along the Aegean coast, artists and architects created magnificent temples and tombs, such as the memorial built for Maussollos, ruler of the Karian city of Halikarnassos.

This diverse world was briefly unified in the fourth century BC, first by Philip of Macedonia, who forcibly united the states of the Greek mainland in 338BC, and then under his son Alexander the Great, who continued into Asia. In an astonishing campaign lasting eight years, Alexander conquered Persia and gained control of a region stretching from Egypt to north-west India, thereby spreading Greek culture over a vast area.

The period between Alexander's death in 323BC and the death of Cleopatra VII of Egypt in 30BC is known as the Hellenistic era. This period witnessed a flowering of

11

13

the arts and culture for a more cosmopolitan society; each dynasty founded
cities and constructed great public
monuments in cities such as Pergamon,
Alexandria and Antioch, while the
individual's needs were catered for by
new religious cults and a rise in private
portraiture and dedications. However,
the Hellenistic world was not blessed
with peace. As the Macedonian empire
dissolved, supremacy was hotly contested
by new superpowers, including Rome,
a culture itself deeply influenced by
Greece. Thus, although the fall of Egypt
to the Romans in 31BC marked the end
of Greek political independence in the
Mediterranean, Greek thought, literature
and art continued to be disseminated
throughout the Roman and Byzantine
empires into medieval times.

14

10 The Nereid Monument,
c. 380BC, from Xanthos,
Lykia, south-west Turkey.
   This tomb building was
erected for a Lykian dynast,
perhaps Arbinas, and
combines Greek and Persian
elements of iconography
and design. The statues
standing between the
columns may represent
Nereids, nymphs of the sea.

11 Colossal portrait statue
from the Mausoleum at
Halikarnassos (modern-
day Bodrum, Turkey),
c. 350BC.
   The Mausoleum was
known in antiquity as one
of the Seven Wonders of
the World.

12 Bronze statuette of
a hunter, probably
Alexander the Great.
Hellenistic, c. 250–100BC.
   Scenes of Greek dynasts
hunting were common
dedications during the
Hellenistic period. This
may be from a small group
showing Alexander, or
one of his successors,
participating in this
heroic activity.

13 Bronze head of a North
African man, c. 300BC.
Found beneath the Temple
of Apollo at Cyrene.
   Greek colonies were
established throughout the
Mediterranean, including
North Africa.

14 Pair of gold disc and
amphora earrings linked
by a long chain. Hellenistic,
300–200BC, said to be
from Egypt.
   After Alexander the
Great conquered Egypt
in 332BC, the jewellery
industry became almost
completely Hellenised,
although jewellery with
Egyptianised details has
been found throughout
the Hellenistic world.

The Roman Empire

According to legend, the city of Rome was founded by Romulus in 753BC. Originally a monarchy, its last King, an Etruscan, was ousted in 509BC, thus marking the beginning of the Republic. Located in central Italy and surrounded by Etruscans, Sabines and Greek settlers, the Romans were exposed to a wide variety of outside influences from the earliest times. The Etruscan influence on archaic Rome is clearly evident in its terracotta and cast-bronze artwork, temple architecture and aristocratic, clan-based society. Another strong influence came from the Greek colonies in Sicily and southern Italy. The Romans worshipped many of the same gods as the Greeks; their alphabet derived from that of the Greeks; they struck coins modelled on Greek prototypes and shared in the economic life of the Greek colonies.

Between the sixth and fourth centuries BC, the Romans slowly extended their power base in Italy through conquest, treaty and alliance. From the third century onwards, however, especially after the defeat of the Carthaginian general Hannibal, their horizons began to expand rapidly. The defeat of Carthage in 146BC left Rome the undisputed mistress of the western Mediterranean. In the same year, Rome destroyed the important Greek city of Corinth and brought under Roman control or influence much of the eastern Mediterranean, with its patchwork of Hellenistic kingdoms suffused with Greek culture.

Closer contact with the Greek world through slaves, hostages and merchants who came to Rome led to a major surge of Greek influence in literature, philosophy and especially the visual arts. Many artists in the Roman world came from the Greek east and were trained in Hellenistic traditions. These traditions, including wall painting, fine architecture and sculpture, and mosaic, had an immediate appeal for the wealthy élites of Rome and other cities, who provided a ready market for all forms of Hellenistic art. Some elements of Roman art, however, retained a distinct identity. Portrait sculpture was particularly realistic, whether statues of statesmen and generals or humbler portraits found on private funerary monuments.

However, the Republic which achieved this unique blend of cultures eventually became a victim of its own success as its leaders' ambition grew. In 49BC, Julius

1

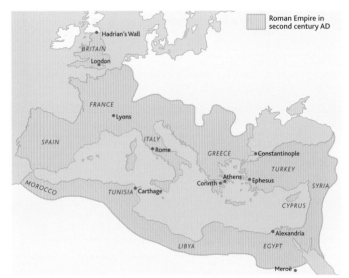

2

Legendary foundation of Rome 753BC

Last Etruscan King of Rome, Tarquin the Proud, deposed
Beginning of the Republic 509BC

900BC   800BC   700BC   600BC   500BC

3

5

4

1	Bronze head of the Emperor Augustus. From Meroë, 27–25 BC.	2	Silver coin. Early Roman, c. 300 BC.	3	Sardonyx intaglio (engraved gem) showing an Imperial lady, possibly Livia, wife of Augustus, as the goddess Diana. 35–27 BC.	4	Funerary monument, 30–10 BC.	5	Painted mummy portrait. From Hawara, Egypt, AD 55–70.

1 Bronze head of the Emperor Augustus. From Meroë, 27–25 BC.

Coins and statues were the main media for propagating the Emperor's image throughout the empire and a continuous reminder of Roman power.

2 Silver coin. Early Roman, c. 300 BC.

Contact with the Greek cities of Sicily and southern Italy led the early Romans to copy their coinage. It was the wealth of these cities, acquired by the Romans during their expansion into Italy, that so changed Roman society.

3 Sardonyx intaglio (engraved gem) showing an Imperial lady, possibly Livia, wife of Augustus, as the goddess Diana. 35–27 BC.

The nobility were often portrayed as deities, and a cult honouring the Emperor and his family spread throughout the Empire.

4 Funerary monument, 30–10 BC.

The subjects are a free-born Roman priest and his wife, a former slave. Among the privileges given by Augustus to freedmen and -women was the right to marry Roman citizens.

5 Painted mummy portrait. From Hawara, Egypt, AD 55–70.

Realistic portraiture was a strong Roman tradition, and mummy portraits of the urban élite illustrate the fusion of different cultures in Egypt as throughout the Empire.

Gallic Celts sack Rome 390 BC	Early Roman coinage from c. 280 BC		218–201 BC Second Punic war with Carthaginians; Hannibal invades Italy and nearly conquers Rome	Caesar's conquest of continental Gaul 58–51 BC	27 BC Augustus declared Emperor; beginning of the Empire
	Rome's first major road built in Italy, the Via Appia 312 BC	290 BC Rome controls all of central Italy	Carthage and Corinth destroyed 146 BC	Expeditions to Britain 55–54 BC	44 BC Julius Caesar murdered
400 BC	300 BC		200 BC	100 BC	0

6

Caesar defeated his rivals and became dictator. The civil war that followed his assassination in 44BC culminated in the defeat of Cleopatra and Mark Antony at Actium and the capture of Egypt. The victor was Octavian, Caesar's nephew and adopted son, who was renamed Augustus and became the first Emperor in 27BC. Rome now controlled the entire Mediterranean region, from Spain in the west to Syria in the east. This culturally diverse empire was held together by the figure of the Emperor: religion, poetry, sculpture, even the writing of history, all reflected his central role.

Although wars continued on the Empire's frontiers, its core was at peace for the first time in many years. This *pax Romana* brought with it unity and stability, resulting in a flourishing of towns and cities and a boom in trade, manufacturing

and the arts. Within the Empire's strong frontiers, *Romanitas*, or Roman-ness, in language, dress, architecture and the arts spread rapidly. The heart of the Empire was its cities, which were broadly similar in form and functions. At the centre of city life was the forum, with basilicas for law-giving, general administration and tax collection, and temples for the worship of the gods. Bathing establishments provided recreation and social interaction, while the arena with its animals, hunters and gladiators, the circus with its chariot races, and the theatre provided the populace with entertainment.

The third century was a period of dramatic change. A succession of weak and short-lived emperors fought civil wars that exhausted the cities and drained Imperial funds. The frontiers of the Empire collapsed under barbarian assaults, and

7

	AD79 Pompeii and Herculaneum buried during eruption of Vesuvius		
Julio-Claudian dynasty AD27–68		Antonine emperors AD117–193	
Roman occupation of Britain AD43	Flavio-Trajanic dynasty AD69–117	c. AD122 Hadrian's Wall begun	AD193–235 Severan emperors
AD50	AD100	AD150	AD200

order was not restored until the reign of Diocletian at the end of the third century. He reorganised the Empire so that the eastern and western halves were separately administered.

The Emperor Constantine changed the course of history when in AD313 he issued the Edict of Milan, which proclaimed Imperial toleration of Christianity. The Christian church could now play an official role in Roman society, and this role grew more important as Constantine and other notable Romans endowed the church with wealth and power. Christian symbolism appeared on mosaics, pottery and silver, though pagan motifs and scenes, long embedded in the popular imagination, remained more common. Other religions that worshipped only one God grew strong in the late Empire, especially that of the Persian god Mithras, particularly popular among soldiers.

In AD330, Constantine moved his seat of government eastwards to Constantinople, which survived as the capital of the eastern or Byzantine Empire for another thousand years. The west of the empire was gradually conquered by barbarians such as the Franks and the Vandals, and in AD410 Rome itself was sacked by the Visigoths. *Romanitas* continued, through language, laws and customs, but the Roman Empire was no more.

8

9

10

6 Marble statue of Mithras, second century AD.

Mithras, whose cult originated in Persia, was one of the eastern deities whose worship spread throughout the Roman Empire during the second and third centuries. Here, he is shown slaying the bull whose blood was believed to have given life to the world.

7 The Portland Vase, as famous for its chequered history as for its superb craftsmanship. Roman, early first century AD.

A masterpiece of cameo glass, the vase probably shows the wedding of Peleus and Thetis, the parents of the Greek hero Achilles.

8 Pottery lamp showing chariot racing in the Circus Maximus. Second–early third century AD.

Around the edges can be seen the heads of the spectators, the starting gates (*carceres*) and the central barrier. At the centre four-horse chariots (*quadrigae*) race around the track. Chariot racing was the oldest form of mass entertainment in the Roman world.

9 Coin portrait of Postumus (AD260–269).

By the mid-third century AD, the Roman Empire was in chaos. In AD261, the Gallic Emperor Postumus, shown here in the guise of Hercules, took advantage of the situation and proclaimed an independent Gallic empire comprising France, Spain, Britain and Germany. With its capital at Trier, it lasted about fifteen years.

10 Gladiator's helmet, first century AD.

Gladiatorial games, in which armed men fought, sometimes to the death, were a popular form of entertainment throughout the Empire. The games were not just about blood. The audience wanted a good show with lots of skill.

AD212 Roman citizenship extended to all free inhabitants of the provinces

AD286 Initial division of Empire under Diocletian

AD395 Final division of the Empire into East and West

Sack of Rome by Visigoths AD410

Deposition of the last Roman Emperor of the West AD476

Freedom of Christian worship recognised under Constantine AD313

AD330 Constantinople consecrated as new Imperial capital

| AD250 | AD300 | AD350 | AD400 | AD450 |

Roman Britain

In AD43, a Roman army of around 40,000 soldiers sailed across the English Channel to Britain. There was resistance to the invasion, but it was soon overcome, and, although military campaigns in the north and west were to continue for many years, the Roman Emperor Claudius was able to travel to Britain to receive the surrender of eleven British kings. Britain had become a province of the Roman Empire.

In fact, there had already been a long period of contact between Britain and the Roman world, but the conquest nevertheless brought about profound changes. For nearly 400 years, Latin was the official language, and Britain's legal and administrative systems and currency were those of Rome. Towns, imposing stone and brick buildings, roads and bridges, classical religion and art all became familiar. The vastly increased choice of everyday goods included many imports, and settlers from other provinces in Europe, the Middle East and North Africa created a richer and more diverse society.

Yet the Roman way of life did not wholly replace the existing British culture, and there was continuity as well as change. The degree of 'Romanisation' varied from region to region and within different communities, but nowhere was the native heritage completely lost or suppressed. Over many generations, the traditions of Iron Age society interacted and combined with classical elements to form a distinctive Romano-British cultural identity.

Britannia was not always peaceful. The province was almost lost in AD60, when Boudica, the widowed queen of the Iceni tribe of East Anglia, led a revolt against the new Roman regime. Even with the construction of Hadrian's Wall

following the Emperor's visit to Britain in AD122, there were periodic disturbances when northern tribes crossed the frontier and raided the province. Hundreds of writing tablets discovered at the Roman fort of Vindolanda near Hadrian's Wall give a vivid glimpse of the garrison in the troubled times preceding the building of the Wall. By the fourth century AD, however, Britain appears to have become a relatively secure and prosperous part of the Empire. The villas of the wealthy reached their peak of opulence, with grandiose buildings and colourful mosaics. Christians, no longer subject to persecution following the Edict of Toleration of the Emperor Constantine in AD312, were able to worship more openly, and evidence of the spread of the religion has been found throughout the province. But religious diversity seems to have continued, and in late Roman Britain there was probably a complex blend of beliefs and practices, some Roman, some native and some of Eastern origin.

Towards the end of the fourth century AD, there were an increasing number of attacks on the province, including the so-called 'Barbarian Conspiracy' of AD367 by the Picts, Scots, Saxons and Attacotti. The government and administration of Britain began to break down, buildings in both town and country started to fall into disrepair, and units of the army were withdrawn from the province. Finally, in AD410, the Emperor Honorius advised the towns of Britain 'to look to their own defence'. There was no mass exodus of 'Romans' – by now the people of *Britannia* were Romano-British. Instead, a gradual but fundamental change in lifestyle occurred as Britain progressively came under the control of Saxons from across the North Sea.

1

AD43 Roman conquest of Britain	AD122 The Emperor Hadrian visits Britain	AD211 Death of the Emperor Septimius Severus at York
AD60/61 Boudican revolt		
AD50 AD100	AD150	AD200 AD2

The Roman Army

The *pax Romana* – the peace that
existed throughout the vast
Roman Empire in the first and
second centuries AD – was
largely dependent on the
efficient army that protected its
borders. Recruited from
throughout the Empire, soldiers
were organised into legions
comprising 3,000 to 6,000
infantrymen supported by cavalry,
military engineers, craftsmen
and administrators. Their
commanding generals were more
often career politicians than
professional soldiers. When not
on campaign, soldiers were
based in forts. The letters and
artefacts recovered from the fort
at Vindolanda, near Hadrian's
Wall, provide insights into the
daily lives of the foreign soldiers
garrisoned there. The letter
shown here is written in ink on
a very thin wooden tablet.

2

3

1   Bronze head from a
colossal statue (one and
a quarter times life-size)
of the Emperor Hadrian
(AD117–38), found in the
River Thames, near the third
arch of London Bridge.
    The statue probably
stood in a public building
or space such as the forum.

2   The head of Christ depicted
in the central roundel of
a large mosaic floor,
fourth century AD, from
a Roman villa at Hinton
St Mary, Dorset.

3   Ink writing-tablet from
Vindolanda fort,
Northumberland.
    A birthday invitation,
written c. AD97–103, from
Claudia Severa to Sulpicia
Lepidina, the wife of the
garrison commander at
Vindolanda. The main part
of the letter was written by
a scribe, but the four short
closing lines at the bottom
right, in Claudia Severa's
own hand, are the earliest
known example of writing
in Latin by a woman from
anywhere in the Roman
Empire.

AD367 Britain attacked by the 'Barbarian Conspiracy'

AD410 End of Roman Britain

AD300   AD350   AD400   AD450

Medieval Europe

Following the collapse of the Roman Empire in the fourth century AD, local ruling classes throughout the provinces were left to themselves to protect their Romanised lifestyle from threats of barbarian invasions and internal discord. One area where a Romanised aristocracy did survive relatively undisturbed was in eastern Europe, where the Byzantine Empire held sway for another thousand years. In the west, however, local 'Romans' faced a troubled future. One approach they adopted was to enlist aid from the barbarians themselves: in Britain, for example, Anglo-Saxon peoples first arrived as mercenaries, though they soon established their own kingdoms, much as other Germanic peoples did in France and Italy.

At the same time, the Christian religion spread classical culture to the Celtic peoples on the western fringes of the former empire and beyond into Ireland, where Latin learning and the associated arts of metalwork, book illumination and sculpture flourished in the early Middle Ages. Irish scholars and missionaries contributed to the development of the newly created kingdoms of Britain and Europe.

Under the patronage of new Anglo-Saxon rulers, Germanic artistic traditions were combined with classical elements to produce the spectacular jewels and weaponry found in wealthy graves such as the seventh-century Sutton Hoo ship burial. Although the conversion of pagan kings to Christianity ended the practice of burying artefacts with the dead, it helped to reunite western Europe, paving the way for a revival of learning in the early ninth century.

By the eleventh century, trade and warfare had led to a consolidation of large kingdoms in western Europe. Viking seafarers from the north had already been active from the Baltic to the Mediterranean. Although their intrusions into mainland Europe were often brief and destructive, Viking settlements in Britain and Ireland stimulated the growth of trade and urban development. Scandinavia, for the first time, was brought into the sphere of Europe.

As the European nations crystallised, common artistic styles developed. Romanesque architecture, typified by round, classically inspired arches and barrel-vaulted ceilings, was adopted for churches and monastic buildings in both

1

2

AD476 Fall of the last Roman Emperor in the West	AD597 Augustine arrives in Kent	Coronation of Charlemagne AD800

AD500   AD550   AD600   AD650   AD700   AD750   AD800   AD

80

3

4

5

| 1 | Byzantine ivory carving. From Constantinople, sixth century AD.

One leaf of an ivory diptych, this carving of the Archangel Michael illustrates the persistence of Greek and Roman traditions in Byzantine art. |
| 2 | Chess-pieces, probably made in Norway, c. AD1150–1200.

Found on the Isle of Lewis, Outer Hebrides, Scotland, the pieces consist of elaborately worked walrus ivory and whales' teeth in the forms of seated kings and queens, mitred bishops, knights on their mounts, standing warders and pawns in the shape of obelisks. |
| 3 | Romanesque gilt-copper and enamel altar cross. Mosan, c. AD1160. |
| 4 | The Londesborough Brooch. Silver gilt set with amber. Irish, mid to late eighth century AD.

One of the finest brooches in the Museum's medieval collection, rich enough to have belonged to a king or church treasury, its history is unknown beyond inclusion in Lord Londesborough's collection. |
| 5 | Tiles depicting Richard I and Saladin. Chertsey, England, c. AD1250–60.

This scene of Saladin receiving a fatal blow from the lance of Richard I has no foundation in fact, since, although they were famous adversaries during the Third Crusade (AD 1189–92), Saladin did not die at Richard's hands. |

c. AD899/900 Death of Alfred the Great

First Crusade takes Jerusalem AD1099

Building of Chartres Cathedral AD1194

AD1215 Magna Carta

Battle of Hastings AD1066

Fourth Crusade takes Constantinople AD1204

AD900 AD950 AD1000 AD1050 AD1100 AD1150 AD1200

northern and southern Europe from the ninth to the twelfth century. The subsequent rise of French power in the thirteenth century coincided with a general trend towards the Gothic style, characterised by pointed arches, rib-vaulted ceilings and more slender proportions. The great Gothic cathedrals of northern Europe well illustrate the new emphasis on ambitious artistic endeavours, although smaller-scale artistic achievements in such disciplines as enamel work and ivory carving are equally eloquent.

Court cultures, built on international dynastic marriages, promoted their own intellectual interests, particularly in the field of literature. Notions of romantic love elaborated by the troubadour poets of eleventh-century Languedoc ultimately developed into a formalised code of conduct that determined aristocratic behaviour. Many of the decorative arts prospered in this atmosphere of luxury. Love tokens in the form of high-status inscribed jewellery were widely circulated,

and deluxe ivory caskets and mirror cases were produced in Parisian workshops in the fourteenth century for sale to aristocratic clients.

Luxury commodities travelled from the East along routes established by Mongol traders. Increased commerce and the higher-density populations of cities, however, had the adverse affect of transmitting disease along these very same routes. The Black Death (or bubonic plague) which periodically dominated the Middle Ages first reached Constantinople in AD1347. Italy, France, Spain, Portugal and southern England all fell victim to the plague during AD1348. Perhaps as much as a third of the population of Europe was decimated in this first outbreak, which continued its course through Scotland and Germany, reaching the Baltic in AD1350.

Cures for infections were routinely sought as much from saints as from doctors, as devotion to the former and veneration of their relics fuelled religious

6

The Sutton Hoo Ship Burial

In 1939, a great barrow excavated at Sutton Hoo in Suffolk yielded a remarkable find: a rich Anglo-Saxon burial contained within the hull of a longship. Among the treasures were large quantities of gold, jewellery and functional items such as weaponry, buckets and a musical instrument. Dated to the seventh century by coins, the burial seems to be that of a local ruler, possibly Redwald, King of the East Angles and overlord of the Anglo-Saxon kingdoms, who died c. AD625. The most spectacular finds included this magnificent iron helmet, a pair of gold shoulder clasps inlaid with garnet and coloured glass, and the gold belt-buckle (no. 6).

sentiment. Relics were collected avidly from the ninth century onwards, and the prestige of individual churches often rested on the status of the relics they possessed. Frequently accommodated in sumptuous shrines and reliquaries, these became the focus of miracle working and pilgrimage. The three most important pilgrimage centres in Europe were Rome, Santiago de Compostella and Canterbury. The most important destination was of course the Holy Land, which lay under Islamic control. The tensions generated by this situation culminated between the eleventh and thirteenth centuries in the Crusades, a series of military expeditions aimed at recapturing Christian holy places in the Near East. The chief effect of the Crusades, however, was to diminish Byzantine power in the region, ultimately leading to the fall of Constantinople in the fifteenth century.

9

7

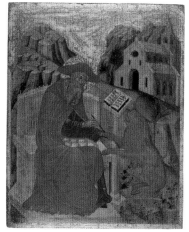

8

6 Gold belt buckle from the ship-burial at Sutton Hoo, Suffolk, England. Early seventh century AD.

The surface of the buckle and the tongue plate are decorated with writhing snakes and intertwining four-legged beasts. Their bodies are highlighted with punched ornament filled with black niello.

7 Silver-gilt figure probably used to decorate a reliquary. English or French, late thirteenth or early fourteenth century.

8 Icon of St Jerome extracting a thorn from the paw of a lion. Probably from Crete, early fifteenth century.

9 The Royal Gold Cup. Enamelled gold, c. AD1380.

A masterpiece of French Gothic art, the Royal Gold Cup was originally made as a gift for Charles V of France, but formed part of the English royal collections in the fifteenth and sixteenth centuries. The decoration shows scenes from the life of St Agnes.

Renaissance & Later Europe

The period extending from the fourteenth century until the death of Michelangelo in 1564 is known as the Renaissance, a time when a renewed emphasis on classical learning was employed as the basis for a humanist interpretation of the universe. Its principles were keenly manifested in the arts of Italy, where Giorgio Vasari's *Lives of the Most Excellent Painters, Sculptors and Architects* (1550) became the basis of a critical framework for the development of European art, reflecting a new status for artists themselves. Albrecht Dürer was a vital point of contact between the culture of northern and southern Europe following his two journeys to Italy in 1494–5 and 1505–7, achieving a personal renown that was symptomatic of the changing status of artists.

The Reformation and the spread of Protestantism in the north had profound implications for religious imagery, taking advantage of the introduction of printing for the propagation of ideas. Successive waves of religious persecution brought about the exile of many important groups of craftsmen: the Protestant Huguenots, for example, who were driven out of France and settled in England from the mid-sixteenth century onwards, included gold- and silversmiths, miniature painters, clockmakers and ivory carvers.

The continuing importance of classical knowledge lay behind the phenomenon of the Grand Tour, an indispensable part of the education of the British aristocracy from the early seventeenth century onwards. Their patronage resulted in the importation of countless antiquities, Old

1

2

3

	Brunelleschi adds dome to Florence Cathedral 1420		1457 First printed book: Mainz Psalter		1506 Bramante rebuilds St Peter's, Rome 1517 Luther publishes his 95 theses	Palladio publishes *Four Books of Architecture* 1570
		Fall of Constantinople 1453	Columbus's first voyage to America 1492		Michelangelo paints Sistine Chapel, Rome 1508–41	Birth of Shakespeare 1564
1400	1425	1450	1475	1500	1525	1550

5

1 Cast-bronze medal of Leon
   Battista Alberti (1404–
   1472) by Matteo de' Pasti
   (fl. c. 1441–68).
      One of the foremost
   scholars and architects of
   the Renaissance, Alberti
   was the author of treatises
   on painting, sculpture and
   architecture.

2 'Nemesis' or 'The Great
   Fortune' by Albrecht Dürer
   (1471–1528), 1501–2.
      The central figure of
   'Nemesis' in this engraving
   is based on the canon of
   proportions derived from
   Vitruvius' classical treatise
   on architecture, a seminal
   text for the Renaissance.

3 'Ideal head of a woman'
   by the sculptor, painter,
   architect and poet
   Michelangelo Buonarroti
   (1475–1564).
      This highly finished
   drawing, dated to the
   second half of the 1520s,
   was intended as a work of
   art in its own right to be
   presented to a patron or
   close friend.

4 Thomas Tompion (1639–
   1713) was one of the most
   celebrated clock- and
   watchmakers in Europe.
   He was at the forefront of
   advances in technology but
   also much in demand for
   timepieces to be used in a
   domestic setting, such as
   this miniature eight-day
   travelling clock in an exceptionally fine silver casing.
   It may have been made
   for a French Huguenot
   customer in England.

5 Maiolica (tin-glazed
   earthenware) bowl by
   Nicola da Urbino.
      Painted c. 1524, this
   bowl is one of a set made
   for the outstanding patron
   and collector Isabella d'Este
   in Mantua, whose arms and
   personal devices appear
   at the centre.

1618 Start of Thirty Years' War in Germany	Last Ottoman attack on Vienna 1683	Foundation of British Museum 1753

Newton publishes *Principia Mathematica* 1687

1600	1625	1650	1675	1700	1725	1750

The Spirit of Inquiry

One of the aspects of the spirit of inquiry fostered by the Renaissance was the desire to provide a systematic classification of all areas of knowledge. This eventually extended to the arrangement of many of the collections that were later absorbed into Europe's major museums. Foremost among these was the British Museum, which was founded by Act of Parliament in 1753 to house the collections of Sir Hans Sloane. A physician by profession, Sloane's lucrative practice enabled him to indulge his great passion for natural science and collecting. He became a Fellow of the Royal Society in 1685, and in 1727 its President in succession to Sir Isaac Newton. On his death, he left (in addition to a library and a herbarium) some 80,000 objects, which included 'things relating to the customs of ancient times or antiquities', coins and medals, and books, prints, drawings and manuscripts. The same impulse to expand the frontiers of knowledge, allied to the trading interests of the European courts, supplied the incentive for geographical exploration; the establishment of additional trade routes and contact with hitherto unknown continents introduced new materials and imagery that had an immediate impact on European culture.

6

Master paintings, prints and drawings, as well as contributing to the growth of Rome and Naples as major artistic centres by the latter part of the eighteenth century. By this stage, the legacy of antiquity, stimulated by new archaeological discoveries, was playing a dynamic role in the evolution of a neo-classical style epitomised by the ceramic wares of Josiah Wedgwood. Wedgwood derived inspiration from the Greek vase collection purchased by the British Museum from Sir William Hamilton, the British Envoy in Naples, in 1772.

In contrast with the decorum of Neo-classicism was the Romantic emphasis on the sublime effects of the relationship between human beings and nature. The early manifestations of the Industrial Revolution combined with the political upheavals of the late eighteenth and early nineteenth centuries to engender a mood of apocalyptic fervour that informed so much of the work of the visionary artist and poet William Blake.

The Napoleonic Wars helped to crystallise nationalist feeling, which gathered momentum throughout Europe in the course of the nineteenth century. In artistic terms, this was often expressed through historical revivalism. For example, the neo-Grecian building designed by Robert Smirke for the Museum was itself linked to a belief that Athens was the cradle of democracy whose legacy was embodied in the British political system. On the other hand, Gothic Revivalism, whose most brilliant exponent in Britain was A.W.N. Pugin, was the style chosen for the design and decoration of the new Houses of Parliament that opened in 1847, because it evoked the spiritual values of the Christian Middle Ages.

7

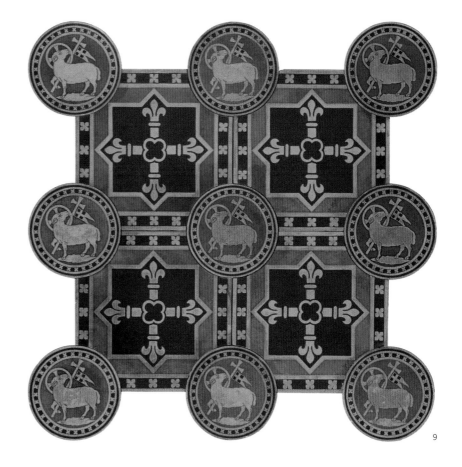

9

8

6 Sir Isaac Newton (1642–1727) by David Le Marchand (1674–1726).

The English mathematician, physicist, astronomer and philosopher Newton personified the spirit of scientific enquiry that characterised the Age of Enlightenment. This ivory bust was carved from life by Le Marchand, a Huguenot ivory carver, in 1718.

7 Plate 8 from 'The Song of Los', 1795, by William Blake (1757–1827).

Throughout the early 1790s, Blake was working on a group of prophetic books of his own invention, combining both text and images, which he printed in colour. The 'Song of Los' ends with this image of Los himself, who represents the creative spirit anxiously awaiting the redemption of man.

8 The Pegasus Vase was presented by Josiah Wedgwood to the Museum in 1786 as a supreme example of the quality of work produced at his pottery, Etruria, in Staffordshire.

The main motif, 'The Apotheosis of Homer', was originally modelled for Wedgwood in 1778 by the sculptor John Flaxman (1755–1862), based on an Athenian red-figured vase in the Hamilton collection.

9 Tile panel from the floor of the Roman Catholic Cathedral of St George in Southwark, London, built between 1841 and 1848.

Designed by the cathedral's architect, A.W.N. Pugin, and manufactured by Minton & Co., the floor incorporates medieval motifs within a highly original design and colour scheme.

Modern Europe & America

During the course of the nineteenth century, the concept of modernity became inseparable from the development of an industrialised urban consumer society, whose advent was most notably proclaimed by the Great Exhibition of 1851 at the Crystal Palace in London. It was impossible for artists, designers or educators to maintain a neutral stance towards the means of production, giving rise, on the one hand, to a desire to harness the principles of good taste to the processes of mass production and, on the other, to the Ruskinian belief in the moral and artistic superiority of handicraft. One of the most innovative designers of the late nineteenth century was a professor of botany, Christopher Dresser, who achieved considerable individuality of expression in all branches of the applied arts, exploiting

new technology with particular success in his metalwork designs. He firmly rejected a Eurocentric historicism in favour of a variety of Japanese, South American and Islamic influences, working with both organic and geometric forms.

Charles Rennie Mackintosh, the architect of the Glasgow School of Art, introduced new structural principles into the design of his buildings and their fittings, which contributed to the evolution of an international Modernist style. However, Mackintosh was not concerned with the democratisation of design through collaboration with industrial manufacture. This issue was addressed in Germany by the activities of the Deutsche Werkbund, founded in 1907, and by the Bauhaus, founded in 1919, and in Scandinavia, whose domestic products

became a byword for high-calibre design that catered for a broad market.

In the fine arts, modernism was allied to the weakening of academic authority and the desire for new forms of expression that would articulate contemporary life. The French Impressionist painters who exhibited as a group between 1874 and 1886 liberated the whole field of artistic endeavour, shifting the emphasis away from the sanction of tradition in favour of the perpetual reinvention of an avant-garde identity. In the twentieth century, there was no more brilliant example of the capacity for constant renewal than Picasso, whose influence as a painter, draughtsman, printmaker and sculptor has been universal.

Expressionism, which developed in Germany in the first decade of the

1

2

3

5

1   Edgar Degas (1834–1917), *Dancers at the Barre*, 1876–7.

Leisure and entertainment were among the main categories of subject matter to which the Impressionists were drawn, and Degas chose the world of the dancers at the Paris Opéra as one of his principal themes. He was attracted not only by the spectacle of performance but also by the private moments backstage or in the practice room, as shown in this study for a painting in the Metropolitan Museum of Art, New York.

2   Electroplated nickel-silver teapot designed by Christopher Dresser in 1879 and made by the firm of James Dixon & Sons, Sheffield.

The teapot copies contemporary Chinese square teapots and was unlike anything made in Western Europe at this date. But it was expensive to make, involving much handwork. This is the only known example.

3   Pablo Picasso (1881–1973), *Study for Les Demoiselles d'Avignon*, 1907.

From autumn 1906 until the following summer, Picasso was immersed in the many studies leading up to the controversial painting *Les Demoiselles d'Avignon*, the cornerstone of modern art. In the form in which Picasso finally left it, the composition contained five female figures, including one related to this figure study.

4   E. L. Kirchner (1880–1938) was the key figure among 'Die Brücke', a group of artists based in Dresden, then in Berlin from 1905–13. Their reinterpretation of the woodcut lay at the heart of the development of the Expressionist style with which they became identified. Among the most striking of all Kirchner's considerable output as a printmaker is this portrait from 1915 of his friend and fellow-artist, Otto Mueller (1874–1930).

5   A clock that formed part of the furnishings designed by C.R. Mackintosh (1868–1928) in 1919 for the guest bedroom of a Victorian terrace house in Northampton which he completely transformed for its owner, the engineering-model manufacturer, W.J. Bassett-Lowke.

	1939–45 Second World War		1969 First moon landing	1989 Collapse of Berlin Wall
1930	1940	1950	1960	1970	1980	1990

twentieth century, provided a highly
charged vocabulary that was especially
appropriate to conveying the sense of
dislocation and trauma created by the
First World War and its aftermath. By
the early 1920s, Expressionism had lost
its appeal for the more radical artistic
factions, who turned variously to devising
anti-rational visual languages such
as Dadaism and Surrealism, or to the
rigorously composed elements of
Constructivism, which the Bauhaus
teacher László Moholy-Nagy described
as 'fundamentals that are without
deceit . . . the socialism of vision'.

The latter part of Moholy-Nagy's
career, like that of so many émigrés from
Germany and Eastern Europe, was spent
in America, which became the major
beneficiary of progressive developments
in Europe between the world wars. With
its exciting industrial and urban imagery
and vast domestic market for consumer
goods, the US had long provided fertile
ground for designers, artists and theoreti-
cians. One of the most influential tracts
of 'Americanism' was the historical study
Mechanization Takes Command, published
in 1948 by the Swiss author Siegfried
Giedion, which became a key text in
Britain for artists such as Richard Hamilton
and Eduardo Paolozzi, who were associated with Pop Art. At the same time, the
assimilation of Cubism, Surrealism and
the pure abstraction of artists such as the
Bavarian-born Hans Hofmann or the
Dutchman Piet Mondrian laid the ground-
work for a quintessentially American
movement, Abstract Expressionism.

From the mid-1960s onwards, a more
assertive European identity emerged,
coupled with a greater eclecticism in art
and design in both the US and elsewhere
that has acknowledged the increasing
pluralism of cultural reference in today's
global society.

6

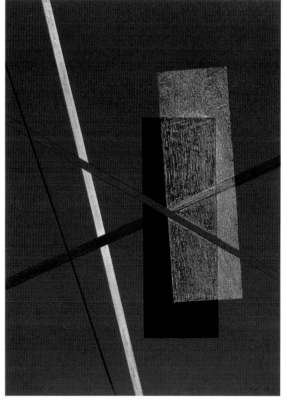

7

8

9

10

6 One of 23 pieces of Russian Revolutionary porcelain made in Petrograd (St Petersburg) in 1921 to raise money for famine victims.

The materials and techniques were the same as those used for luxury items under Tsarist rule, but the vocabulary was new, creating a dynamic design from the lettering and dating in the centre of the plate, surrounded by wheat ears, a traditional symbol of famine or plenty.

7 The portfolio of lithographs executed by László Moholy-Nagy (1895–1946) in 1923 remains one of the purest expressions of Constructivist values in the field of printmaking. His principal interests lay in photography, typography and industrial design which he pursued as both a practitioner and a theoretician at the Bauhaus and then through the School of Design that he opened in Chicago in 1939.

8 A silver-plated hot water urn designed in 1934 by the Finnish architect Eliel Saarinen (1873–1950) for the Cranbrook Academy of Art, Michigan.

Saarinen was one of a number of influential European émigrés who helped to promote modern design in America. Cranbrook Academy owed much to the earlier Bauhaus in Germany, with workshops for metal, textiles and ceramics.

9 *Ulysses*, James Joyce's modernist masterpiece first published in 1922, has haunted Richard Hamilton's imagination since 1947. The etching and aquatint *In Horne's House* was completed in 1982 to mark the centenary of Joyce's birth. Its subject, the emergence of different artistic styles, including objects from the collections of the British Museum, is a visual parallel to Joyce's use of the birth of a child as a metaphor for the birth of the English language.

10 *Terror.Virtue*, by Ian Hamilton Finlay (b. 1925) with Nicholas Sloan. Cast bronze, Scotland, 1984.

This medal turns an autobiographical episode (a confrontation between the artist and Strathclyde Regional Council) into a political statement, attacking bureaucratic mismanagement over the centuries since the French Revolution. The columns stand for virtue, while the visually similar guillotine represents state oppression.

Conservation

It is not enough for museums to collect, document, research, store and display fascinating objects: they must do all they can to prevent them decaying further. The use of the word *further* is deliberate, because it is a law of nature that every object starts to decay from the moment it is produced. However, efforts can be made to slow down the rate of decay, and it is the function of the Museum's conservation department to do this. There are two basic ways in which this can be achieved: by intervening directly ('active conservation') or by providing the best possible environment so that decay processes are reduced to a realistic minimum ('passive conservation').

Conservation has been practised in one form or another since the earliest days at the Museum. The earliest practitioners were craftsmen who had taught themselves to make and restore objects. The need for special methods came into focus in 1845, when the Portland Vase was smashed into approximately 200 pieces in an act of vandalism. A museum craftsman, Mr Doubleday, was given the task of repairing the vase, and he did an excellent job, it being necessary to repeat the task only in 1948 and then in 1989.

These three dates are of interest in that they represent different phases in the state of conservation attitudes and techniques. In 1845, there were no specialists, and Doubleday was untrained. By 1948, there were 'craftsmen restorers' working as professionals, but no vocational

1

2

3

courses were available, and they learned their skills at the bench. There are no records of how the Portland Vase was conserved in 1845 or 1948. In 1989, however, the whole process was closely documented, and a film was made of it. By this time, all conservators were receiving specialist training and working within a Department of Conservation which had been set up in 1975.

Many conservators today need to be highly specialised. For example, there are specialist conservators for cuneiform tablets, coins and papyrus rolls. All objects included in permanent and temporary exhibitions are examined prior to display by conservators who ensure that they are stable enough to be displayed inside glass cases. The materials from which cases are constructed have to be tested to ensure that they are not themselves the source of unacceptable pollution. The galleries have to be checked to make sure that light levels are not too high, causing colours to fade and objects to fall apart. The atmosphere itself must not create dangers, and humidity, temperature, dust levels and pollution are measured (they can now be monitored remotely). Not infrequently, Museum conservators are assigned to archaeological excavations, where on-site conservation may be vital for the survival of newly discovered objects. The processes of conservation are demanding, but the Museum has a responsibility to ensure that objects are available not only for our own generation but for hundreds of years to come.

4

5

1 Nigel Williams conserving the Portland Vase in 1989. Because the adhesive used in the previous restoration was deteriorating, the vase was dismantled into its 200 or so separate pieces and reassembled using modern adhesives.

2 A recently excavated, highly decorated horse bit, from Sutton Hoo, is carefully cleaned by Fleur Shearman.

3 A humidity gauge is checked in an exhibition gallery by David Thickett.

4 Close-up of the final retouching process being undertaken by Mitsuhiro Abe on the eighteenth-century Toyoharu screen.

5 Fibres of a fragmentary papyrus being realigned by Bridget Leach to make the document legible.

Scientific Research

When we look at an object in the British Museum, it can give an immediate impression of some aspect of the day-to-day life of its makers or users – what they drank or ate from, the gods they believed in, even what they looked like. Beyond appearance, however, lies an abundance of other information, which can only be obtained through the use of sophisticated scientific equipment. The Museum supports scientific laboratories staffed by research scientists whose mission is to complement more traditional curatorial studies in better understanding the collections and to enhance their preservation.

Many of the objects illustrated in this guide have been subjected to detailed scientific examination. X-radiographs, of the type familiar from visits to hospital, are used to see beneath the surfaces of objects. These may help to elucidate the techniques used by early smiths to construct outstanding pieces of metal-work such as the Royal Gold Cup or reveal the watermarks in the paper of Old Master drawings. Lasers, X-rays and sophisticated microscopes can show that the appearance of an object has been dramatically modified by the vagaries of time. Traces of pigment on sculptures from the Parthenon provide vital clues to their original colour scheme, while detailed analysis of ancient metalwork can allow us to see beyond the effects of centuries of corrosion.

Modern chemical analysis can provide detailed insights into the ways in which objects were obtained and used. Clay may be fingerprinted by the traces of metals it contains, so that ceramic vessels like Italian maiolica and Korean celadon may be assigned to the regions, or even the kilns, where they were made. Traces of organic material in the surface of a pot may indicate the type of food that was cooked in it, or the oil that it held.

Things are not always what they seem, and science has a long history in the unmasking of forgeries. Authenticity remains an important issue for the Museum, but it is not simply a question of condemning fakes. It may be a matter of demonstrating that an unusual arte-fact, without clear parallels, is genuinely old. For example, in 2001, with the help of the Heritage Lottery Fund and National Art Collections Fund, the Museum was able to acquire a unique gold Celtic warrior brooch at a cost of about a million pounds. Detailed examination in the Museum's laboratories had demon-strated beyond reasonable doubt that the brooch was everything it purported to be, thus allowing the purchase to be made with confidence.

2

1

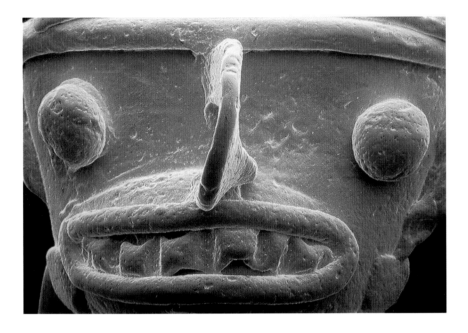

3

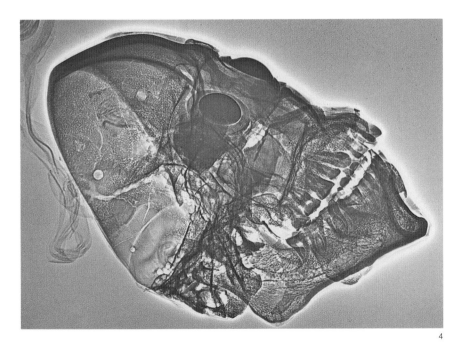

4

5

1. Careful examination of an Egyptian figurine (left) under the microscope, coupled with X-ray fluorescence and diffraction techniques, allows the reconstruction of its original appearance (right).

2. In the scanning electron microscope, we can see clearly the lion engraved on a Mesopotamian cylinder seal and tell that it was cut with a jeweller's wheel.

3. A gold pendant from Panama.

(Left) Examination of this head from a gold pendant in the scanning electron microscope shows that it was made by lost-wax casting.

4. A radiograph reveals the human skull used as a form for an Aztec turquoise mosaic (no. 5).

5. Turquoise-mosaic mask of the creator-god Tezcatlipoca, 'Smoking Mirror'. Mixtec-Aztec, AD1400–1521.

The Aztec court commissioned skilled Mixtec artisans to produce lapidary work of the highest order, notably mosaic masterpieces.

Support the British Museum

The British Museum needs and values your support: please do everything you can to help us in at least one of the ways outlined below.

Books and gifts
A wide range of books on archaeology, art, history and ethnography is published by the British Museum Press, a division of the British Museum Company. The British Museum Company also offers an attractive selection of unusual gifts and other goods based on the collections of the British Museum. To view books and gifts online, request a catalogue or place an order, visit the British Museum Company website at: www.britishmuseum.co.uk

You can also join the free mailing list, request catalogues or order goods on the following numbers:
Tel. from the UK: 0800 085 0864;
from overseas: +44 (0)20 7637 1292
Fax: +44 (0)20 7436 1382
Email: customerservices@bmcompany.co.uk

Shops
Within the Great Court are the main bookshop, the souvenirs and guides shop and the children's shop. The Grenville shop, situated off the Front Hall of the Museum, sells jewellery, fine silks and sculpture. There are also shops outside the Museum at 22 Bloomsbury Street (200 m from the Great Russell Street entrance to the Museum) and at Heathrow Airport, Terminal 4 (airside). For enquiries, please telephone: +44 (0)20 7323 8584

Travel
The British Museum Traveller (fully bonded, ATOL 3090) runs art, archaeology, history and ethnography tours, led by expert guides, to sites and cities around the world. For a brochure please contact The British Museum Traveller:
Tel.: +44 (0)20 7436 7575
Fax: +44 (0)20 7580 8677
Email: traveller@bmcompany.co.uk
www.britishmuseumtraveller.co.uk

The British Museum Friends
Since starting in 1967 the British Museum Friends have raised over £2 million to support the work of the Museum. Members of the Friends enjoy free entry to exhibitions, a lively calendar of exclusive activities including the monthly 'First Tuesday' late night gallery talks, free subscription to the Museum magazine and advance notice of all museum-wide events. Friends also get exclusive use of a suite of beautiful rooms in the old curatorial East Residence of the British Museum. In addition the shops and restaurants offer a 10% discount on all purchases. For more information please contact:

The British Museum Friends
The British Museum
Great Russell Street
London WC1B 3DG
Tel.: + 44 (0)20 7323 8605
Fax: + 44 (0)20 7323 8985
Email: friends@thebritishmuseum.ac.uk

American Friends of The British Museum
The American Friends (a 501(c)(3) charity) raises awareness and financial support for the British Museum in the United States. Contributions are tax-deductible within the limits prescribed by law. A variety of membership categories and giving opportunities are available. For more information please contact:

American Friends of The British Museum
One East 53rd Street, 12th Floor
New York
NY 10022
Tel.: +1 212 644 0522
Fax: +1 212 644 0509
Email: info@afbm.org
www.afbm.org

The British Museum Development Trust
As the British Museum looks forward to the rest of the twenty-first century, it is undergoing one of the most radical transformations in its history. Needless to say, raising the necessary funds to realise the new plans is an enormous challenge. There are various ways of supporting the wide range of projects at the Museum and we at the British Museum Development Trust would welcome the opportunity to discuss them with donors.

INDIVIDUAL DONATIONS
The British Museum is an institution fortunate in knowing individuals who share our passion for collecting, for scholarship and for ensuring that the galleries are accessible and enjoyed by all. We are able to do more as a result of their support and we work hard to ensure that our supporters receive the information, involvement and recognition that they request. The British Museum is a charity under schedule 2 of the Charities Act 1993, which means that donors may receive tax relief as a result of their gifts to the Museum.

PATRONS OF THE BRITISH MUSEUM
As a Patron of the British Museum, your support will help fund the key activities of curatorial research, conservation and education, helping to ensure that the Museum's collections continue to inspire and enlighten our visitors. Patrons enjoy a close relationship with the Museum and are invited to become more involved with our work according to their personal interests. There are several opportunities to meet other Patrons and enjoy the Museum's collections and displays throughout the year.

CORPORATE PARTNERS OF THE BRITISH MUSEUM
As a Corporate Partner of the British Museum, your company will enjoy a mutually beneficial relationship with the Museum, including opportunities for corporate hospitality, talks in the workplace and free entrance for employees to paying exhibitions.

A PLACE IN YOUR WILL FOR THE BRITISH MUSEUM?
By leaving a gift in your Will, you are enabling the Museum and its collections to inspire future generations. Legacies and bequests contribute to the work of the Museum, through funding for scholarships, conservation, research and education. Your gift can take the form of money or assets, an object, a single work of art or a collection.

For more information, please contact:
The British Museum Development Trust
91 Great Russell Street
London WC1B 3PS
Tel.: +44 (0)20 7636 5765
Fax: +44 (0)20 7636 5779
Email: development@thebritishmuseum.ac.uk

ILLUSTRATION ACKNOWLEDGEMENTS

All the photographs are by the British Museum Photographic Service and are ©The Trustees of The British Museum, with the exception of the following:

p. 7 Towneley Hall Art Gallery and Museums, Burnley Borough Council; p. 89 Pablo Picasso, *Seated Nude*, 1907, © Succession Picasso/DACS 2003; E.L. Kirchner, *Portrait of Otto Mueller*, 1915, © Ingeborg and Dr Wolfgang Henze-Ketterer, Wichtrach/Bern; p. 90 László Moholy-Nagy, *Construction I*, 1923, © DACS 2003; p. 91 *In Horne's House*, 1982, © Richard Hamilton; *Terror.Virtue*, 1984, © Ian Hamilton Finlay.

Maps by ML Design
Museum plans by Jeffery Design and Nigel Coath